A Manager's Guide to
Employee Privacy
Laws, Policies, and Procedures

A MANAGER'S GUIDE TO
EMPLOYEE PRIVACY
LAWS, POLICIES, AND PROCEDURES

Kurt H. Decker

WILEY

John Wiley & Sons, Inc.
New York • Chichester • Brisbane • Toronto • Singapore

Publisher: Stephen Kippur
Editor: David Sobel
Managing Editor: Ruth Greif
Editing, Design, & Production: Publications Development Co.,
Crockett, Texas

This publication is designed to provide accurate and authoritative information in regard to the subject matter covered. It is sold with the understanding that the publisher is not engaged in rendering legal, accounting, or other professional service. If legal advice or other expert assistance is required, the services of a competent professional person should be sought. FROM A DECLARATION OF PRINCIPLES JOINTLY ADOPTED BY A COMMITTEE OF THE AMERICAN BAR ASSOCIATION AND A COMMITTEE OF PUBLISHERS.

Library of Congress Cataloging-in-Publication Data

Decker, Kurt H.
      A manager's guide to employee privacy:
      laws, policies, and procedures/ Kurt H. Decker

ISBN 0-471-50903-5

Printed in the United States of America

89 90 10 9 8 7 6 5 4 3 2 1

For Hilary, Christian, Allison, and Martina
our "personlike feline,"

the ones in my life
where "privacy" is most
cherished, enjoyed,
and understood

PREFACE

One of the most rapidly evolving areas of employment law involves employee privacy interests. Employers are confronted with new or revised privacy requirements that necessitate regular review of their procedures and policies.

To meet these employee privacy challenges, this book outlines procedures, policies, and forms for guiding employees, employers, human resource professionals, and attorneys. The book reviews each employee privacy interests: (1) general principles, (2) procedures relevant in implementing or maintaining it, and (3) policies for applying it.

Chapter 1 presents an audit procedure for employers to use in evaluating their overall employee privacy needs. **Chapters 2** through **8** cover specific employee privacy interests that arise during hiring, at the workplace, and outside the workplace by examining privacy issues present in: (1) initial employment contacts, (2) employment data verification, (3) records, (4) medical concerns, (5) information collection, (6) personal workplace concerns, and (7) those outside the workplace.

This book synthesizes into practical procedures, policies, and forms the general principles of employee privacy set forth in K. Decker, *Employee Privacy Law and Practice*, published by John Wiley & Sons, Inc. (1987). This book can be consulted whenever legal principles relevant to a particular employee privacy issue should get a more in-depth perspective.

The procedures, policies, and forms that are presented in this text should only be considered guidelines. They should not be adopted verbatim or applied without careful evaluation. Many require careful review of applicable employee privacy legal considerations that are continuously subject to revision. Each should be considered as it applies to a particular employer's needs and requirements before being implemented. Once adopted, they should be consistently followed. If they cannot be followed, they should be discontinued or revised to reflect what actually exists.

Reading, Pennsylvania   KURT H. DECKER

ACKNOWLEDGMENTS

In preparing this text, many individuals either provided opportunities or shared their knowledge. Those who provided research materials or thoughtful discussion were H. Thomas Felix II, Esquire, of Sprecher, Felix, Visco, Hutchison, and Young in Philadelphia, Pennsylvania for his initial review of this manuscript; Joseph E. Herman, Esquire of Seyfarth, Shaw, Fairweather & Geraldson's Los Angeles, California office for permitting adaptation of his employee relations audit materials; Arbitrator, John M. Skonier for his encouragement; James Troebliger, Manager of Human Resources of GPU Nuclear Corporation for his input regarding alcohol and drug abuse procedures; and Dr. Edwin M. Wagner of Saint Francis College for allowing me to present these developing employee privacy principles to industrial relations graduate students. Above all, this project would not have been undertaken without the foresight of Edward B. MacGuire and David Sobel at John Wiley & Sons, Inc. who early on recognized the emerging importance of employment privacy issues for attorneys and human resource professionals.

K.H.D.

CONTENTS

CONTENTS

ALPHABETICAL LIST
OF FORMS

1

EMPLOYEE PRIVACY ISSUES
AND CONCERNS

Increasingly, employers are recognizing the potential liabilities
created by the growth and expansion in employment litigation
arising out of individual employee rights. What was once limited to disputes occurring under grievance arbitration procedures in collective bargaining agreements has changed; any
adverse employment decisions of private and public sector employers can be subject to prolonged court litigation and costly
damage awards or settlements, and federal and state agency
regulation.

Failing to recognize potential employee privacy problem
areas can have negative employer litigation implications. Employer litigation exposure can be minimized by understanding
potential employee privacy liability arising

1. Out of hiring,
2. At the workplace,
3. Outside the workplace.

To assess your potential liability, a systematic means must
be developed for defining current privacy interrelationships
between employees and their employers and for measuring
changes that have occurred in these privacy relationships. Employee privacy audits provide an employer with a method for
reviewing and evaluating employer exeosure and liability
potential. The employee privacy audit includes an initial questionnaire, a review of relevant employer documents, discus-
sions with management and supervisors, supplemental written
inquiries, and an evaluation.

For an employee privacy audit to be useful, honest and

accurate employer responses must be given, even though legal concerns may be raised in identifying potential employee privacy liability. These responses are essential for pinpointing and isolating employee privacy problem areas so that preventive action to minimize these issues and concerns can be taken before they create employer liability. The human resources staff should coordinate the audit function.

This chapter reviews employer procedures for assessing employee privacy liability potential. It examines the issues and concerns present, privacy audit formats, and privacy audit result analysis, along with human resource administration responsibilities and employee privacy discipline considerations.

ISSUES AND CONCERNS

RECOGNIZING EMPLOYEE PRIVACY ISSUES AND CONCERNS

Employment law trends regarding individual employee rights protection mandate that employers take preventive measures to minimize their litigation potential arising out of employee privacy claims. Employers must evaluate the strengths and weaknesses of their employee privacy procedures and policies in order to identify problem areas. Although some of these privacy problem areas may be apparent, other deficiencies may be overlooked. Recognizing these issues and concerns may require consultation with legal counsel and human resource professionals to assure that employer procedures and policies comply with applicable federal and state statutes.

To identify employee privacy issues and concerns, information must be collected from a variety of sources. Once collected, the information can be assembled and reported on employee privacy audit forms for evaluation. In collecting this information, the employer must obtain an understanding about its own structure, internal organization, communication, human resource administration, recruitment, work hours, compensation, fringe benefits, promotions and transfers, fair employment practices, discipline, termination, and leaves of absence, union relations, health and safety, training and development, and manpower planning.

Employer Structure

To evaluate potential employer liability for privacy intrusions, the employer's overall structure should be examined. Regarding privacy, this may reveal employer philosophy and sensitivity, as well as confidentiality considerations present in developing, manufacturing, and marketing products or services. In undertaking this, the following should be considered:[1]

1. Date operations commenced
2. Acquisition and/or merger involvement that may affect employee privacy interests by inheriting conflicting procedures and policies
3. Products
4. Facility location
5. Annual revenue:
   - Current year
   - Prior year
   - Five years ago
6. Number of employees by job classification:
   - Currently
   - One year ago
   - Two years ago
7. Private or public ownership
8. Sales to government agencies
9. Competitors
10. Union organization:
    - Which unions?
    - For how long?
    If not unionized, have attempts been made to organize?
    - Which unions?
    - When?
    - Results?

---

[1] Adapted from Littler, Mendelson, Fastiff & Tichy, *Conducting a Labor Relations Self Audit: An Outline for Examining Personnel Policies and Practices* in The 1987 Employer H-2 to H-3 (1987).

A broad-based labor relations audit is conducted for employers by Littler, Mendelson, Fastiff & Tichy to pinpoint employment liability areas out of its California offices (located in Fresno, Los Angeles, Palo Alto, Sacramento, San Diego, San Francisco, San Jose, and Walnut Creek) and in Baltimore, Maryland, hereinafter referred to as "Littler." Littler, Mendelson, Fastiff & Tichy prepare this publication on an annual basis for Business Laws, Inc. of 8228 Mayfield Road, Chesterland, Ohio 44025; telephone (216) 729-7996. As an annual update of employment law, this is an excellent reference source for human resource professionals and attorneys.

Internal Employer Organization

To understand how employee privacy procedures and policies are emphasized and stressed, the employer's organization becomes important. Employer organization is important for recognizing the responsibility for developing, implementing, and communicating employee privacy procedures and policies, along with their dissemination through a human resource function. The following should be considered regarding the employer's organizational structure:[2]

1. Organization chart
2. Job position descriptions:
   - Clearness
   - Accuracy
   - Completeness
   - Availability
   - Development responsibility
   - Regular updating
3. Organization structure:
   - Appropriateness for meeting employee privacy goals
   - Checks and controls
   - Overlapping authority
   - Authority commensurate with responsibility
4. Organization function:
   - Employee quality for administering privacy procedures and policies
   - Employee knowledge of privacy procedures and policies
   - Employee understanding of privacy relationships
   - Decision level at which employee privacy procedures and policies are formulated and implemented
   - Acceptance of employee privacy procedures and policies throughout the organization

Communication Methods

To ensure that employee privacy procedures and policies are understood by managers, supervisors, and employees, communication is important. Through communication, employee

---

[2] Adapted from Littler at H-4 to H-5.

privacy procedures and policies are disseminated within the employer's organization. Communication assures knowledge, understanding, and consistent application of privacy procedures and policies. The following should be considered regarding communication:[3]

1. Providing employee privacy information
2. Support and encouragement for internal employee privacy procedures and policies
3. Informing managers and supervisors of employee privacy procedures and policies, along with interpretations of those procedures and policies
4. Consistent application of employee privacy procedures and policies
5. Encouraging employees to express views and reactions to employer interpretations of privacy procedures and policies
6. Providing a procedure for reviewing and resolving non-union employee privacy complaints
7. Encouraging participation by managers and supervisors in implementing employee privacy procedures and policies
8. Effect on employee privacy procedures and policies of:
    * Turnover
    * Cooperation
    * Privacy complaints
9. Bypassing managers and supervisors when implementing employee privacy procedures and policies
10. In-house newsletters or similar publications to communicate employee privacy procedures and policies
11. Letters or other written documents to communicate employee privacy procedures and policies
12. Suggestion system to review employee privacy concerns
13. Receptiveness to employee privacy concerns and issues

Human Resource Administration

To implement employee privacy procedures and policies properly, responsibility for this within the employer's organization must be assigned. Administration is important for consistency

<hr />

[3] Adapted from Littler at H-5 to H-6.

in developing, implementing, applying, interpreting, and communicating privacy procedures and policies. Generally, this responsibility rests with those individuals involved with the human resource administration function. The following should be considered regarding human resource administration:[4]

1. Existence of a human resource staff or similar personnel function:
   - Number of employees
   - Annual budget
   - Organization
   - Reporting responsibility
   - Ratio of overall employees to the human resources staff

2. Legal and/or professional organization membership for learning of employee privacy developments

3. Professional information and journals received for access to employee privacy developments

4. Legislative information reviewed for updating employee privacy requirements

5. Human resource staff assistance in solving employee privacy issues and concerns

6. Human resource staff solicitation of privacy needs and information from managers and supervisors before developing privacy procedures and policies

7. The human resource staff as a pro-active or re-active employer function to employee privacy issues and concerns

8. Existence of an employment handbook

9. Existence of a personnel record for each employee regarding its:
   - Contents
   - Impermissible identification of employees by race, color, religion, sex, national origin, ancestry, physical handicap, age, or marital or veteran status
   - Employer maintenance of any record regarding an applicant's or employee's race, color, religion, sex,

---

[4] Adapted from Littler at H-6 to H-9.

national origin, ancestry, physical handicap, age, or marital or veteran status for use in legal reporting

- Record changes in employee status involving promotions, leaves of absence, rates of pay, and so forth

10. Providing employees with document copies that affect their employment status

11. Employee access to personnel records

12. Employer personnel record use for:
    - Hiring
    - Transfers
    - Promotions
    - Performance reviews
    - Disciplinary action
    - Staff review
    - Employment statistic development

Recruitment

The recruitment process plays an important role in employee privacy hiring considerations. When seeking employment, an individual must provide considerable personal information and allow the employer to verify it. Recruitment creates vast employment information resources through employee disclosures, medical examinations, testing, interviews, and background investigations. It affects employee privacy interests present in beliefs, speech, information, and association. Because of this, the following should be considered regarding recruitment:[5]

1. Recruitment:
    - Present employee considerations
    - Recruitment programs
    - Recruitment sources used:
        —Advertising
        —Internal referrals
        —Employment agencies
        —Executive search
        —Other sources

[5] Adapted from Littler at H-9 to H-13.

2. Selection:
   - Selection methods used:
     — Preliminary screening
     — Interview by: human resources staff, supervisor, or staff psychologist
     — Testing by: test description and test validation
     — Reference investigation
     — Credit investigation
     — Arrest and criminal record investigation
     — Education verification
     — Pre-employment physical examination
   - The selection method's appropriateness
   - Providing applicants information about the employer, the position, and career potential
   - Employment applications regarding:
     — Providing the applicant with a copy
     — Any questions or specifications pertaining to race, color, religion, sex, national origin, ancestry, physical handicap, age, or marital status
   - Pre-employment physical examinations
   - Requiring persons to be bonded
   - Applicant or employee photographs
   - Applicant or employee submission to polygraph examinations, drug screening, or similar tests
   - Employee identification badges
   - Communicating selection determinations to candidates regarding:
     — Acceptance
     — Rejection
3. Candidate evaluation procedures involving:
   - Initial screening
   - Technical skills
   - Psychological examination
4. Job offers regarding:
   - Hiring decisions
   - Offer procedures
   - Employment offer follow-up
   - Monitoring outstanding employment offers

5 Familiarizing new employees through:
- Orientation program
- Employee handbook

6. Recruiting staff:
- Number
- Qualifications
- Consistency of recruiting plans with the employer's needs

Work Hours

Employee privacy intrusions may originate out of work hours. These intrusions arise through the variety of personal attributes and problems that employees bring into the workplace, which must be molded into productivity. This assimilation process must take place while preserving employee association, speech, belief, and lifestyle interests at the workplace. The following should be considered regarding work hours:[6]

1. Normal workday hours
2. Normal workweek hours
3. Normal workweek days
4. Shifts operated
5. Starting times
6. Quitting times
7. Work hour recording
8. Overtime work:
- Assignment
- Overtime equalization
- Employer notification of assigned employees
- Employee refusal to work overtime
9. Attendance control
10. Outside employment restrictions

Compensation

Employee privacy intrusions may originate in compensation through this information's collection, maintenance, use, and

---

[6] Adapted from Littler at H-13 to H-14.

disclosure. Compensation and the confidentiality surrounding it may be one of the more personal employee privacy issues. It can affect one's associations and the perceptions that others have. Collecting, maintaining, or disclosing inaccurate compensation information is possible because each employer has its own recordkeeping system. Regarding compensation, the following should be considered:[7]

1. Deductions withheld
2. Deduction authorization
3. Use of itemized statements setting forth deductions
4. Attendance records
5. Time off for voting
6. Time off for jury or witness duty
7. Accepting employee wage assignments
8. Procedures and policies regarding payment to employees who resign
9. Procedures and policies regarding payment to terminated employees
10. Job descriptions for:
    - Managerial
    - Supervisory, administrative, and technical/professional
    - Nonexempt salaried
    - Hourly
11. Job description updating reflecting:
    - Existing job changes
    - New jobs
12. Job description format concerning:
    - Responsibilities
    - Authority
    - Reporting relationships
    - Titles
    - Qualifications
13. Job description use in:
    - Evaluating jobs
    - Recruiting

[7] Adapted from Littler at H-14 to H-20.

- Organization planning
- Counseling

14. Job description release
15. Preparing and maintaining job description responsibility
16. Job classification base pay ranges
17. Wage range determination
18. Job evaluation
19. Job reevaluation or updating frequency
20. Wage surveys
21. Compensation program administration
22. Responsibility level at which compensation decisions occur
23. Performance reviews:
   - Employees covered
   - Frequency
   - Responsibility
   - Feedback
   - Supervisor training in reviewing performance
   - Performance reviews in relation to pay increases
   - Performance evaluation checklist or guide
   - Performance review measurement of job performance
   - Performance review criteria establishment
   - Performance criteria communication to employees
   - Formal means of relating compensation to job performance
   - Appropriate relationship between compensation and job performance
   - Wage increases based solely on merit
   - Wage rate review frequency
   - Wage increase determination
   - Receipt by employees in the same pay range of the same merit increase
   - Performance review discussion by supervisors with employees
   - Performance review data use in management development, training, and manpower planning
   - Human resource staff involvement
   - Performance review data confidentiality
   - Employee wage rate data confidentiality

Fringe Benefits

Employee privacy claims may arise out of fringe benefits when information communication received from use of the benefits discloses intimate facts about the employee.[94] This may occur when sensitive employee medical information is revealed, for example. Disclosure of this information may affect employee speech and associational interests. The following should be considered regarding fringe benefits:[8]

1. Life insurance
2. Hospitalization, surgical, and medical
3. Sickness and accident
4. Major medical
5. Disability
6. Dental
7. Optical
8. Travel accident
9. Pension/retirement
10. Savings plan
11. Stock purchase
12. Credit union
13. Paid holidays
14. Leaves of absence
15. Paid vacations
16. Educational reimbursement
17. Length of service
18. Other forms of fringe benefits

Promotions and Transfers

Promotions and transfers may involve employee privacy concerns that arise out of testing affecting beliefs, speech, and associations. For employers, a desire exists to fill available positions with employees qualified for the tasks assigned. Tests may deny employment to minorities without evidence that the tests were

[8] Adapted from Littler at H-20 to H-23.

related to job success. Because of this, the following should be considered regarding promotions and transfers:[9]

1. Tests the employer uses to determine employee promotion eligibility
2. Test validation
3. Test access to all employees
4. Communication to employees of job openings and tests
5. Selection criteria for choosing between employees with equal qualifications and abilities

Fair Employment Practices

Various employee privacy claims may arise out of federal and state fair employment practices (FEP) statutes. These statutes may become relevant when employment decisions are made and/or information is collected, maintained, or disclosed regarding race, color, sex, religion, national origin, handicap, or marital status. These FEP privacy considerations may be present at hiring, in the workplace, and outside the workplace. Incorrect collection, maintenance, use, or disclosure may affect employee privacy interests present in beliefs, speech, and association. Because of this, the following should be considered regarding FEP:[10]

1. Employer policies against discrimination because of race, color, religious creed, sex, national origin, ancestry, physical handicap, age, or marital status in:
   - Hiring
   - Promotions
   - Transfers
   - Salary increases
   - Work assignments
   - Other
2. Written FEP policies
3. Communication to employees
4. Employer commitment in demonstrating opposition to discriminatory and harassing employment practices

[9] Adapted from Littler at H-23 to H-24.
[10] Adapted from Littler at H-24 to H-25.

5. The human resource staff's and supervisors' familiarization with and action in conformity to FEP statutes
6. Advertisements, applications, or interviews containing any specifications regarding race, color, religious creed, sex, national origin, ancestry, physical handicap, medical condition, age, or marital status
7. FEP policy communication to employment agencies
8. Minority group employment
9. Administration responsibility
10. Government contract involvement
11. Affirmative action plans and goals
12. Female and minority distribution at each employer responsibility level
13. History regarding discrimination complaints, conciliations, outstanding or pending lawsuits, or other FEP actions

Discipline, Termination, and Leaves of Absence

Frequently, employee privacy claims and liability arise out of discipline, termination, or leaves of absence. Many privacy injuries occur during the hiring process or before an employment termination. While employed, the adversely affected employee must usually suppress privacy objections to retain employment. Privacy-related litigation usually occurs after termination, when the employee is no longer economically dependent on the employer.

Preventive procedures that consider employee privacy areas may minimize employer liability. Because extensive liability may arise out of discipline, termination, and leaves of absence, the following should be considered:[11]

1. Discipline:
   - Written conduct rules and:
     — Communication to employees
     — Consistent rule interpretation and application
     — Rule enforcement responsibility
   - Employee discipline responsibility
   - Employee discipline imposition absent written conduct rules

---

[11] Adapted from Littler at H-25 to H-29.

2. Employment separation:
   - Separation for:
     — Resignation with notice
     — Resignation without notice
     — Resignation by mutual agreement
     — Termination
     — Layoff
     — Retirement
     — Overstaying leave of absence
     — Failure to return from leave of absence
   - Termination documentation
   - Documentation responsibility
   - Employee turnover record responsibility
   - Turnover rate:
     — Currently
     — One year ago
     — Two years ago
   - Exit interviews conducted for terminating employees regarding:
     — Conduct
     — Interview's nature
     — Result utilization
   - Terminated employee record retention
3. Termination procedures:
   - Type of termination procedure
   - Prior to terminating employees, consideration of:
     — Length of service
     — Personnel file documentation
     — Wage increases
     — Promotions
     — Commendations
     — Work criticism
     — Prior discipline or warnings
   - Responsibility for terminating employees
   - Review of termination decisions by higher-level management or human resources staff prior to implementation

- Review by legal counsel
- Procedures for adjudicating employee disputes
- Employer determination that a termination occurs in accordance with its procedures and policies
- Employer guidelines for achieving consistent standards in employee terminations
- Employer oral or written promises to employees regarding employment termination
- Employer notice to employees that their employment is at-will

4. Layoffs:
   - Employee selection for layoff
   - Employee selection for recall

5. Leaves of absence:
   - Leave types:
     — Personal
     — Medical
     — Pregnancy
     — Work-related disability
     — Bereavement
     — Military
     — Jury duty
   - Paid leaves
   - Treatment of employees who fail to return from leaves of absence
   - Treatment of employees who overextend leaves of absence without permission
   - Treatment of employees who work elsewhere during leaves of absence without authorization
   - Procedure for granting leaves
   - Effect of employee's leave on status, seniority, benefits, and so forth
   - Reinstatement of employees to their previous position upon returning from leaves of absence

Union Relations

Where collective bargaining agreements exist, unions may play an important role in the development and administration of employee privacy procedures and policies. Associational rights can be impacted by restricting the employee's right to organize under private and public sector labor relations statutes. Interference with union organizational or associational activities can result from employer surveillance. Refusal to bargain can result from introduction of testing or surveillance devices without consultation or bargaining with an employee representative. A union's right to information also impacts privacy interests. For these reasons, the following should be considered regarding union relations:[12]

1. Number of employees:
    - Supervisory
    - Nonsupervisory
    - Hourly
    - Salaried
2. For unionized employees:
    - Bargaining unit
    - Union's name
    - Relationship length
    - Collective bargaining agreement's expiration date
    - Union membership extent
    - Representation election certification
    - Relations with employees
    - Relations with the union
    - Side agreements, oral or written
    - Past practices between the employer and the union
    - Employer representatives in negotiations
    - Collective bargaining agreement settlements after a strike
    - Step at which most grievances are settled
    - Number of annual grievances
    - Number of annual arbitrations for each unit
    - Union shop clause
    - Check-off for dues and/or initiation fees
    - Unauthorized walk-out experience
    - Unfair labor practice experience

[12] Adapted from Littler at H-29 to H-30.

3. For nonunion employees:
    - Complaint or grievance procedure availability
    - Groups that have attempted to organize
    - Representation election history
    - Majority by which unionization was defeated
    - Work stoppage experience
    - Unfair labor practice experience

Health and Safety

Employee privacy interests may be affected by workplace health and safety. A privacy-related right may arise in the employee's reasonable expectation to be free from workplace hazards or not to have one's physical condition unnecessarily queried. This privacy expectation may involve safety concerns, smoking, alcohol and drug abuse, acquired immune deficiency syndrome (AIDS), sterilization, and so forth. The following should be considered regarding health and safety matters:[13]

1. Safety program
2. Furnishing employees with safety equipment, such as shoes, glasses, and so forth
3. Management and supervisory personnel's knowledge
4. Worker compensation claim experience
5. Providing rooms for resting
6. Retention of a physician's services
7. Use of an industrial nurse
8. Maintenance staff looking for, documenting, and repairing possible unsafe conditions before accidents occur
9. Arrangements with a medical clinic for handling emergencies

Training and Development

To ensure proper implementation, communication, and understanding of employee privacy procedures and policies, training and development involving management, supervisors, and employees must occur. Training is essential to acquaint managers,

---

[13] Adapted from Littler at H-30 to H-31.

supervisors, and employees with what information can be collected, maintained, used, or disclosed, as well as with what employee activities can be legitimately regulated at and outside the workplace. The following should be considered regarding training and development as they relate to privacy procedures and policies:[14]

1. New employees:
   - Orientation program
   - Materials provided
2. Current employees:
   - Continued training
   - Apprenticeship programs
3. Supervisors:
   - Training provided regarding:
     — Responsibilities
     — Structure and operations
     — Role
     — Supervisorial/managerial skills
     — Job requirements
     — Employee relations
   - Other in-house training
4. Management development:
   - Training management
   - Formal training program
   - Program content
   - Program instruction
   - Determining management training needs and program content
   - Outside program use
   - Determining program use responsibility
   - Evaluating training program results

Manpower Planning

To ensure consistent development, as well as quality development of employee privacy procedures and policies, manpower

[14] Adapted from Littler at H-31 to H-33.

planning is important. This planning is important for the proper collection, maintenance, use, and disclosure of employment information. Through this planning, employer liability can be minimized or prevented. The following should be considered regarding manpower planning as it relates to privacy procedures and policies:[15]

1. Staffing:
    - Number of open positions
    - Competence level
    - Understaffing
    - Overstaffing
    - Backup personnel
2. Planning techniques:
    - Employer objectives:
    — Short-term
    — Long-term
    - Planning criteria appropriateness for determining employer needs
    - Workforce forecasts
    - Planners' cooperation with department heads
    - Plan updating frequency
3. Implementation:
    - Planning authority
    - Control mechanisms
    - Planning feedback
    - Coordination with:
    — Internal placement
    — External recruiting
    — Management development

PRIVACY AUDITS

Once employee privacy issues and concerns are recognized, an employee privacy audit can be considered, planned, and conducted. The audit provides a written record of the issues and concerns affecting employee privacy. To perform an employee

---

[15] Adapted from Littler at H-33 to H-35.

privacy audit, forms are provided, which may be used separately or as a whole, to evaluate the employer's privacy procedures and policies in areas involving: (1) background information; (2) recruitment, hiring, and workforce composition; (3) job descriptions, assignments, promotions, and transfers; (4) employer communications; and (5) discipline and termination.

BACKGROUND INFORMATION AUDIT FORM

This audit form should be used in obtaining an understanding regarding the employer's philosophy, product, services, growth, and operations. It also indicates what employment information is being collected, maintained, used, and disclosed.[16]

---

[16] Adapted from J. Herman, Employee Relations Audit Questionnaire 4 (Seyfarth, Shaw, Fairweather & Geraldson, Apr. 15, 1984), hereinafter referred to as "Herman." A broad-based employee relations audit is regularly conducted for employers by Seyfarth, Shaw, Fairweather & Geraldson, to pinpoint employment liability areas, out of its offices located in Los Angeles, California; San Francisco, California; Washington, D.C.; Chicago, Illinois; and New York, New York.

BACKGROUND INFORMATION AUDIT FORM

1. Attach an organizational chart of the employer's operations.

2. List all employer facilities, their location, the number of supervisory employees, and the number of nonsupervisory employees employed at each facility along with describing each facility's function.

Facility/ Location	Supervisory Employees	Nonsupervisory Employees	Total Function

3. For each facility, specify the number of employees represented by a union, the union's name, and the date of the union's recognition or certification.

Facility	Employees	Union's Name	Date of Recognition or Certification

Attach copies of current collective bargaining agreements.

4. For each facility, list all departments, indicating the person responsible for supervising the department and all job classifications/titles, indicating the number of employees in each classification.

Department	Supervisor	Job Classifications	Employees

Attach any organizational charts.

5. List the name, job title, and duties of the person who has direct responsibility for employment relations procedures and policies at each facility and the length of time that position has been held.

Name	Job Title	Duties	Time Position Held

6. Identify whether written employer procedures and policies are used for implementing the following:

	Yes	No
a. Fair Employment Practices (FEP)	___	___
b. Fair Labor Standards Act (FLSA)	___	___
c. National Labor Relations Act (NLRA)	___	___
d. Age Discrimination in Employment Act (ADEA)	___	___
e. Occupational Safety and Health Act (OSHA)	___	___
f. Employee Retirement Insurance Security Act (ERISA)	___	___
g. Handicapped employment	___	___
h. Employee privacy federal and state statutory matters	___	___
i. Employment record collection, maintenance, use, and disclosure	___	___

Attach copies of existing procedures and policies relating to the above.

7. Have any facilities been reviewed or investigated by the following governmental agencies:

		Yes	No
a.	The Equal Employment Opportunity Commission (EEOC)	___	___
b.	A state Equal Employment Opportunity Commission (EEO)	___	___
c.	The Department of Labor (DOL)	___	___
d.	A state Wage & Hour Commission	___	___
e.	The National Labor Relations Board (NLRB)	___	___
f.	Occupational Health and Safety Administration (OSHA)	___	___
g.	Any other federal or state agency	___	___

If the answer is yes to any of the above, set forth the following:

Date	Agency and Subject	Result
_____	_____	_____
_____	_____	_____
_____	_____	_____
_____	_____	_____
_____	_____	_____

8. Has any facility ever been subject to a conciliation or settlement agreement with:

		Yes	No
a.	The Equal Employment Opportunity Commission (EEOC)	___	___
b.	A state Equal Employment Opportunity (EEO) Commission	___	___
c.	Department of Labor (DOL)	___	___
d.	A state Wage & Hour Commission	___	___
e.	The National Labor Relations Board (NLRB)	___	___
f.	Other federal or state agency	___	___

9. Has any facility ever been a party to a court decree in a matter involving adverse employment practices?

    ___ Yes   ___ No

    If yes, attach a copy of any decree.

10. Is the following information collected and retained for each employee:

		Yes	No	Time Retained
a.	Employee's full name	___	___	_____
b.	Employee's address, including zip code	___	___	_____
c.	Employee's birth date	___	___	_____
d.	Source of the employee's job opening knowledge	___	___	_____
e.	Employee's employment application	___	___	_____
f.	Employee's hiring date	___	___	_____
g.	Employee's race	___	___	_____
h.	Employee's sex	___	___	_____
i.	Employee's occupation or job classification	___	___	_____
j.	Time and day when the employee's workweek begins	___	___	_____
k.	Employee's regular rate of pay such as "$3.65 an hour," "$200 a week," "piecework," and so forth	___	___	_____
l.	Hours worked by the employee each work day	___	___	_____
m.	Total hours worked by the employee each workweek	___	___	_____
n.	Employee's daily or weekly straight time wages	___	___	_____
o.	Employee's total overtime compensation for the workweek	___	___	_____
p.	Total additions or deductions from wages paid to the employee each pay period	___	___	_____
q.	Total wages paid the employee each pay period	___	___	_____
r.	Date of payment and the pay period covered by the payment	___	___	_____
s.	Date and amount of promotion or demotion received by the employee	___	___	_____
t.	Date of any disciplinary action, including termination, taken against the employee	___	___	_____
u.	Date and description of any employee work-related accidents	___	___	_____
v.	Contact for the employee in case of emergency	___	___	_____

    w. Social Security Number   ___ ___ _____

    x. Other employee information   ___ ___ _____

    Describe:

_____

_____

_____

11. Is the following information disclosed internally or to outside third parties for each employee:

		Yes	No	If Disclosed, Explain
a.	Employee's full name	___	___	_____
b.	Employee's address, including zip code	___	___	_____
c.	Employee's birth date	___	___	_____
d.	Source of the employee's job opening knowledge	___	___	_____
e.	Employee's employment application	___	___	_____
f.	Employee's hiring date	___	___	_____
g.	Employee's race	___	___	_____
h.	Employee's sex	___	___	_____
i.	Employee's occupation or job classification	___	___	_____
j.	Time and day when the employee's workweek begins	___	___	_____
k.	Employee's regular rate of pay such as "$3.65 an hour," "$200 a week," "piecework," and so forth	___	___	_____
l.	Hours worked by the employee each workday	___	___	_____
m.	Total hours worked by the employee each workweek	___	___	_____
n.	Employee's daily or weekly straight time wages	___	___	_____
o.	Employee's total overtime compensation for the workweek	___	___	_____
p.	Total additions or deductions from wages paid to the employee each pay period	___	___	_____
q.	Total wages paid the employee each pay period	___	___	_____

    r. Date of payment and the pay period
covered by the payment   ____ ____ _____

    s. Date and amount of promotion or demotion
received by the employee   ____ ____ _____

    t. Date of any disciplinary action, including
termination, taken against the employee   ____ ____ _____

    u. Date and description of any employee
work-related accidents   ____ ____ _____

    v. Contact for the employee in case of
emergency   ____ ____ _____

    w. Social Security Number   ____ ____ _____

    x. Other employee information   ____ ____ _____

    Describe:

    _____

    _____

    _____

    _____

12. Is the information set forth at questions 10 and 11 maintained on a computer system?

    ____ Yes   ____ No

13. Are employees provided with the records set forth at questions 10 and 11 on request?

    ____ Yes   ____ No

14. Who has access to personnel files?

    _____

15. Describe procedure for updating employee addresses.

    _____

16. Are notices relating to the following statutes or subjects posted in conspicuous places in each facility?

		Yes	No
a.	The Civil Rights Act of 1964 (Title VII)	____	____
b.	The Fair Labor Standards Act (FLSA)	____	____
c.	The Age Discrimination in Employment Act (ADEA)	____	____
d.	The Occupational Safety and Health Act (OSHA)	____	____

    e. Applicable state wage and hour laws   ___ ___

    f. Workers' Compensation carrier's name   ___ ___

    g. Unemployment benefits   ___ ___

    h. Other required federal and state statute notice
postings   ___ ___

    Describe:

    _____

    _____

    If yes, where are these notices posted? _____

17. Are employees provided with each wage payment an itemization of all deductions, dates of period compensated, employer's name, employee's name/Social Security number?

    ___ Yes   ___ No

18. Are EEO-1 reports filed annually?

    ___ Yes   ___ No

19. Does a written affirmative action program (AAP) exist for each facility?

    ___ Yes   ___ No

    If yes, attach copies of the AAPs for the past five years.

20. If there is a written fair employment practice policy, attach a copy and indicate whether the written policy is:

		Yes	No
a.	Included in an employee handbook	___	___
b.	Posted on employee bulletin boards	___	___
c.	Published in a newsletter, annual report, and so forth	___	___
d.	Communicated to all recruiting sources	___	___
e.	Included on all purchase orders, leases, and contracts	___	___
f.	Communicated at regularly scheduled employee meetings	___	___
g.	Communicated to manager and supervisor trainees	___	___
h.	Communicated to managers and supervisors	___	___
i.	List other places where the statement is published:		

_____

_____

_____

_____

RECRUITMENT, HIRING, AND WORKFORCE COMPOSITION
AUDIT FORM

This audit form identifies the employee privacy interests that may be infringed upon during recruitment, hiring, and after hiring as they affect employee benefits, associations, speech, and information.[17]

Note that item 35 may be required under federal and state FEP statutes.

[17] Adapted from Herman at 11.

RECRUITMENT, HIRING, AND WORKFORCE COMPOSITION AUDIT FORM

1. List all oral and written sources in which each facility advertises for employees. Attach a copy of any advertisement used within the last year.

   _____

   _____

   _____

2. Do the advertisements indicate any preference, limitation, or specification based on race, color, religion, age, sex, national origin, or physical condition?

   ____ Yes ____ No

3. Does the oral or written advertising source used by any facility segregate advertising by sex?

   ____ Yes ____ No

4. Do the advertisements indicate a preference for young applicants or place a limit on the years of experience which the applicant may have?

   ____ Yes ____ No

5. Do the advertisements indicate that the employer is an "Equal Opportunity Employer"?

   ____ Yes ____ No

6. List any high schools, trade schools, or colleges at which each facility recruits.

   _____

   _____

   _____

7. Does any facility recruit at organizations/institutions comprised solely of one sex?

   ____ Yes ____ No

8. During the application process, are inquiries made about an applicant's:

		Yes	No
a.	Credit rating	____	____
b.	Marital status	____	____
c.	Garnishment record	____	____
d.	Prior arrest record	____	____

e. Prior conviction record   —— ——
f. Ability to be bonded   —— ——
g. Bankruptcy record   —— ——
h. Charges or complaints filed with any governmental agency   —— ——
i. Workers' compensation claims   —— ——
j. Number of children   —— ——
k. Union affiliations   —— ——
l. Ability to speak/write a foreign language   —— ——
m. Marital status   —— ——
n. Disabilities   —— ——
o. Prior addresses   —— ——
p. Religion   —— ——

9. Does any facility employ an outside investigator/agency to verify applicant information?

    ——— Yes ——— No

10. Are investigative or consumer reports used during the hiring process?

    ——— Yes ——— No

    If yes, specify source:

    _____

    _____

    _____

11. Are applicants notified that investigative/consumer reports will be used?

    ——— Yes ——— No

12. Are qualifications for job positions in writing prior to being advertised?

    ——— Yes ——— No

13. Do the hiring criteria for any job include a limitation on an applicant's:

		Yes	No
a.	Race	——	——
b.	Sex	——	——
c.	National origin	——	——
d.	Religion	——	——
e.	Age	——	——
f.	Height	——	——

g. Weight ___ ___
h. Education ___ ___
i. Marital status ___ ___
j. Place of residence ___ ___
k. Sexual persuasion, homosexuality ___ ___
l. Physical handicap ___ ___
m. Pregnancy ___ ___
n. Military service ___ ___
o. Organizations, activities ___ ___
p. Filing a charge with any governmental agency ___ ___
q. Ability to speak English ___ ___

14. Is any preference given to applicants who are:

                                                      Yes   No

a. Related to present or former rank-and-file employees ___ ___
b. Related to present or former managers or supervisors ___ ___
c. Referred by present or former employees ___ ___

15. Describe the employer's policy regarding hiring present employee relatives.

_____

_____

_____

16. Describe the steps used in processing job applicants.

_____

_____

_____

17. List all individuals responsible for hiring employees.

_____

_____

_____

18. Are any physical, manual, written, verbal, or other tests used in the applicant selection process?
___ Yes ___ No

If yes, attach a copy or description of each test used.

19. Are written job applications used?
    ____ Yes   ____ No

    If yes, attach copies of the applications used.

20. Are employees required to sign applications?
    ____ Yes   ____ No

21. Are applicants required to take a polygraph, honesty, or similar test?
    ____ Yes   ____ No

22. Are applicants required to provide a photograph prior to an interview?
    ____ Yes   ____ No

23. Are applicants advised of the full range of job openings?
    ____ Yes   ____ No

24. For any job position, is there a preference for a particular sex?
    ____ Yes   ____ No

25. Are any employment limitations imposed on persons with young children?
    ____ Yes   ____ No

    Describe if limitations:

    _____

26. Is there a preferred age range for any job?
    ____ Yes   ____ No

    If yes, specify classifications and qualifications:

    _____

    _____

27. What is each facility's policy regarding hiring pregnant applicants?

    _____

    _____

28. Are physical examinations required for applicants?
    ____ Yes   ____ No

    If this examination is not required for all applicants, specify for which categories:

    _____

    _____

29. Is the examining physician provided with a description of the job to be performed by the applicant?

    ____ Yes ____ No

30. Does each facility have the power:

	Yes	No
a. To recruit its own applicants?	____	____
b. To hire new employees?	____	____

    Specify individuals who have the right to hire and their location:

    Person   *Title*   *Location*

    _____

    _____

    _____

31. Does any policy exist regarding applicants proving legal residency?

    ____ Yes ____ No

    If yes, describe policy: _____

    _____

32. How is legal residency verified?

    _____

33. How are applicants informed that they will not be offered a position?

    _____

    _____

34. Define the geographic area from which applicants come.

    _____

35. For each facility, provide the following information, if it is readily available:

    a. Estimated minority population in the immediate labor area.

       _____

    b. Estimated minority percentage of the workforce in the immediate labor area.

       _____

    c. Estimated size of the minority unemployment force in the immediate labor area.

_____

    d. Explain what labor area is used for this data.

_____

_____

36. Are employees required to sign restrictive covenants, nondisclosure of trade secrets, or noncompetition agreements____ Yes ____ No

If so, attach a copy of this agreement(s).

JOB DESCRIPTIONS, ASSIGNMENTS, PROMOTIONS, AND
TRANSFERS AUDIT FORM

This audit form assists in identifying workplace employee privacy intrusions arising out of job descriptions, assignment, promotions, and transfers.[18]

---

[18] Adapted from Herman at 19.

JOB DESCRIPTIONS, ASSIGNMENTS, PROMOTIONS, AND TRANSFERS AUDIT FORM

1. Are written job descriptions maintained?

   ____ Yes ____ No

   If yes, attach copies.

   If no, explain how employees are informed of their specific responsibilities.

   _____

   _____

   _____

   _____

2. Are there any job classifications which contain criteria relating to a person's physical attributes; i.e., weight, height, appearance, and so forth?

   ____ Yes ____ No

3. Are females excluded from any job categories because of state protective legislation regarding hours worked, work type, or weight-lifting restrictions?

   ____ Yes ____ No

   If yes, list categories:

   _____

   _____

   _____

   _____

4. Describe the employer's policy for accommodating employees who cannot work specified days of the week or hours of the day.

   _____

   _____

5. Are there any jobs which employees over age 40 are unable to perform?

   ____ Yes ____ No

   If yes, list these jobs and explain why employees over age 40 cannot perform them.

   _____

   _____

   _____

JOB DESCRIPTIONS, ASSIGNMENTS, PROMOTIONS, AND TRANSFERS AUDIT FORM *(Continued)*

6. Is there a minimum age for employment?

   ___ Yes ___ No

   If yes, what is that age? _____

7. What benefits are given nonunion employees on the basis of their seniority?

   _____

8. How is seniority determined?

   _____

   Is age or sex used in determining seniority?

   ___ Yes ___ No

   If yes, explain use.

   _____

9. When determining job assignments and transfers, are the following factors considered?

		Yes	No
a.	Age	___	___
b.	Sex	___	___
c.	Race/Ethnic origin	___	___
d.	Handicap	___	___
e.	Union membership	___	___

   If yes to any factor, explain its use.

   _____

   Are records made of this?

   ___ Yes ___ No

   If yes, where are they kept?

   _____

10. Has employment in any job, lines of progression, or departments been based on:

		Yes	No
a.	Race	___	___
b.	Sex	___	___
c.	Age	___	___
d.	Handicap	___	___

11. Is a seniority system presently maintained which is based on service during the period when certain jobs, lines of progression, or departments were so segregated?

____ Yes ____ No

12. Are employees permitted to transfer into jobs in lines of progression or departments from which they were formerly excluded?

____ Yes ____ No

13. Are vacant job positions advertised or announced to current employees?

____ Yes ____ No

If yes, are records maintained of who applies for these jobs?

____ Yes ____ No

14. Are records maintained reflecting the reasons for denying or awarding a job to a current employee?

____ Yes ____ No

If yes, describe:

_____

15. How does the employer determine whether an employee should be permitted to move into another position?

_____

_____

16. Are any of the following factors used in determining whether an employee will move to another job?

		Yes	No
a.	Race	____	____
b.	Sex	____	____
c.	Age	____	____
d.	Handicap	____	____

If yes to any factor, explain its use.

_____

_____

17. Are any jobs, lines of progression, or departments limited to persons of one sex?

____ Yes ____ No

18. Are supervisory personnel required to submit written decisions and reasons when employees are passed over for promotions?
____ Yes ____ No

19. Are employees promoted or transferred between facilities?
____ Yes ____ No

    If yes, how often does this occur? _____

    _____

20. For each job classification, describe the training programs used, indicating any employee participation prerequisites.

    Training Program   *Participation Prerequisites*

    _____

    _____

21. Describe procedures for evaluating employee performance.

    _____

    _____

    If a form is used, attach.

22. How frequently are performance evaluations conducted?

    _____

    _____

23. Are performance evaluations reviewed by anyone other than the person who prepared the evaluation?
____ Yes ____ No

24. Describe procedures for reviewing performance evaluations with employees.

    _____

25. Describe the training that supervisors receive regarding employee performance evaluations.

    _____

    _____

EMPLOYER COMMUNICATIONS AUDIT FORM

This audit form identifies how the employer communicates employee workplace privacy procedures and policies.[19]

---

[19] Adapted from Herman at 33.

EMPLOYER COMMUNICATIONS AUDIT FORM

1. Does the employer have an orientation program for acquainting new employees with privacy procedures and policies?

    ____ Yes   ____ No

    If yes, list the privacy subjects discussed and the documents presented to a new employee. Attach copies of booklets or other documents which are given to new employees.

    _____

    _____

2. If there is an orientation program, list the persons responsible for or who participate in the program.

    _____

    _____

3. Are employees required to sign a document acknowledging receipt of an employee handbook or similar document?

    ____ Yes   ____ No

    If so, attach copy of acknowledgment.

4. When was the employee handbook last revised?

    _____

    By whom was the handbook revised?

    _____

5. Is there an employer/facility newsletter?

    ____ Yes   ____ No

    If so, attach copies for past year.

6. What is the employer's policy regarding employee bulletin board use?

    _____

    _____

7. Has the employer conducted surveys among employees during the past five years?

    ____ Yes   ____ No

    If yes, when was the last survey conducted? Who conducted the survey? Attach a copy of the questionnaire and the responses.

    _____

8. Are there any committees composed entirely or partially of employees?

   _____ Yes _____ No

   If so, describe the committee's composition and purpose.

   _____

   _____

9. Are there any regularly scheduled meetings between employees and supervisors?

   _____ Yes _____ No

10. How do employees bring their privacy complaints or concerns to the attention of managers and supervisors?

    _____

    _____

11. What procedures are used by managers and supervisors for responding to employee privacy concerns or complaints?

    _____

    _____

12. Are there any procedures by which an employee may appeal decisions of supervisors?

    _____ Yes _____ No

DISCIPLINE AND TERMINATION AUDIT FORM

This audit form identifies the procedures and policies for resolving employee privacy disputes that may arise at hiring, at the workplace, and outside the workplace regarding discipline and termination, with a view towards limiting employer liability.[20]

Item 5 in this form is concerned with "progressive discipline" which is generally considered an escalating set of steps, imposing more severe discipline for each succeeding employer rule violation by an employee, that eventually culminates in termination. These disciplinary steps may consist of an oral warning, written warning, suspension, and termination.

[20] Adapted from Herman at 40.

DISCIPLINE AND TERMINATION AUDIT FORM

1. Are there any written rules of conduct?
   ____ Yes ____ No

2. When and how are employees informed of employer rules?

   _____

3. Who is responsible for enforcing employer rules?

   _____

4. Do persons responsible for enforcing rules have any discretion in determining the disciplinary penalty to be imposed once it is determined that
   an offense has occurred?
   ____ Yes ____ No

5. Is there any procedure for progressive discipline?
   ____ Yes ____ No

6. How are managers and supervisors informed of the employer's disciplinary procedure?

   _____

7. How and when are employees made aware of the disciplinary procedure?

   _____

8. Are disciplinary decisions made by supervisors reviewed?
   ____ Yes ____ No

9. How and when are employees informed of a decision to discipline them?

   _____

10. Prior to being disciplined, is an employee given an opportunity to present
    his or her explanation?
    ____ Yes ____ No

11. Are employees given the opportunity to discuss the reasons for disci-
    plinary actions against them?
    ____ Yes ____ No

    If yes, please explain.

    _____

    _____

DISCIPLINE AND TERMINATION AUDIT FORM *(Continued)*

12. Are employees allowed to appeal disciplinary actions; i.e., to a higher-level manager or panel of officials?

    ___ Yes ___ No

    If yes, please explain the appeal procedure.

    _____

13. Is an employee who is being investigated to determine whether discipline is appropriate, or who is being notified of a disciplinary decision, permitted to have a person of his or her choice present at the investigation or negotiation meeting?

    ___ Yes ___ No

    If yes and there are exceptions, explain exceptions.

    _____

    _____

14. If an employee receives one or more warnings or negative evaluations, are any of the following measures taken to remedy the problem:

		Yes	No
a.	Upward or downward vertical transfer to place the employee in a position more closely suited to his or her abilities?	___	___
b.	Lateral transfer to alleviate possible personality conflicts between the employee and immediate supervisor or between the employee and fellow workers?	___	___
c.	Additional employee job training?	___	___
d.	Other?	___	___

15. Who is responsible for terminating employees?

    _____

    _____

16. Describe the procedure for documenting disciplinary decisions and the reasons for the decision.

    _____

17. Is age or race ever used as a factor in a decision to terminate employees?

    ___ Yes ___ No

    If yes to any of the above factors, explain its use.

    _____

18. Is sex ever used as a factor in a decision to terminate employees?
    ____ Yes ____ No

    If yes, explain when and how sex is used as a factor.

    _____

    _____

    _____

19. Is a terminated employee allowed to appeal to a higher-level manager or panel of officials?
    ____ Yes ____ No

    If yes, please explain the appeal procedure.

    _____

    _____

    _____

20. Are employees provided with a written termination notice?
    ____ Yes ____ No

21. When are terminated employees given a final paycheck?

    _____

    _____

22. Are terminated employees eligible for severance pay?
    ____ Yes ____ No

23. Are exit interviews conducted?
    ____ Yes ____ No

    By whom? _____

24. Are records maintained of all disciplinary actions, including termination?
    ____ Yes ____ No

25. If yes, describe what records are maintained and where they are maintained.

    _____

    _____

    _____

DISCIPLINE AND TERMINATION AUDIT FORM *(Continued)*

26. Are copies of warnings and terminations placed in the employee's personnel file?

____ Yes ____ No

27. Do warnings contain the following:

		Yes	No
a.	Offense	____	____
b.	Action necessary for improvement	____	____
c.	Consequences of failure to improve	____	____

PRIVACY AUDIT RESULTS

IMPLEMENTING AUDIT CHANGES

After the employee privacy audit has been completed, the following list should be considered in compiling results for further employer action. The employer should be prepared to remedy privacy procedure and policy deficiencies. The audit itself will help you to pinpoint deficiencies, however, once identified, steps must be taken to remedy those deficiencies.

1. The employee privacy audit report should:
    - Identify employee privacy priorities
    - Distinguish facts versus opinions
    - Evaluate employee privacy alternatives
    - Assess employee privacy vulnerabilities
    - Identify confidentiality problems
2. Implement employee privacy changes by:
    - Avoid overreaction
    - Consider gradual versus immediate changes
    - Publicize changes
    - Use employee committees
    - Involve the union (if there is one)
    - Coordinate
    - Provide overall versus specific changes
    - Review the effects
    - Consider new contract provisions where collective bargaining agreements are involved
3. Establish employee privacy monitoring systems regarding:
    - FEP statutory compliance
    - Union activities
    - Health and safety
    - Reporting and recordkeeping
    - Management responsiveness
    - Employee development
    - Disclosure restrictions

EMPLOYEE PRIVACY OVERALL GUIDELINES

The goal of any employee privacy audit should be the development of overall employer privacy procedures and policies. There are some general guidelines that can be used to prevent or minimize employer liability for privacy intrusions. Overall privacy guidelines should include:

1. Consistently applying and following privacy procedures and policies
2. Knowing employee privacy rights under applicable federal and state statutes
3. Making certain that management and supervisory personnel know the applicable law, as well as employer procedures and policies involving employee privacy
4. Making it a policy for employees to refrain from commenting or disclosing information that could affect employee privacy interests involving hair style, religion, politics, spouse, sexual habits, or other sensitive areas
5. Respecting employee rights to privacy and confidentiality
6. Reviewing employee privacy procedures and policies annually to ensure that they are consistent, conform to applicable statutes, and reflect the employer's philosophy
7. Avoiding spontaneous action or action taken in anger
8. Providing employees with some form of due process prior to implementing adverse employment actions by:
   - Taking no adverse employment action without evidence
   - Giving the employee an opportunity to present counter-evidence prior to a final adverse employment action
   - Treating all adverse employment actions consistently
   - Establishing an appeal method for adverse employment actions through internal or external procedures
   - Giving the employee an opportunity to review, comment on, and copy any written performance evaluations or personnel file memoranda pertinent to the adverse employment action
   - Telling the employee why the adverse employment action is being taken
   - Making certain that appeal procedures for adverse employment actions are known and available to all employees

Employers should be aware that employee privacy issues and concerns can confront even the most careful, ethical, and innocent employer. Potential employee privacy claims can be anticipated by periodically updating procedures and policies to reflect the employer's operation and current statutory requirements. At a minimum, updating will safeguard employers against incurring liability that may damage the employer's business.

HUMAN RESOURCE ADMINISTRATION

HUMAN RESOURCE ADMINISTRATION OF PRIVACY RESPONSIBILITIES

Regarding employee privacy procedures and policies, the human resources staff should have the following responsibilities:

1. Preparing procedure and policy recommendations
2. Coordinating and facilitating planning by and among management and supervisors that is necessary for the orderly accomplishment of privacy procedure and policy objectives
3. Continuously reviewing the employer's progress in achieving privacy procedure and policy goals
4. Consulting with employees, supervisors, and managers in determining the feasibility of any privacy procedures and policies
5. Conducting and coordinating research as may be necessary and desirable to develop and implement effective and efficient privacy procedures and policies
6. Conducting studies and analyses of the actual or potential short- and long-term effects regarding present or proposed privacy procedures and policies
7. Assisting in reviewing federal and state actions affecting privacy procedures and policies
8. Serving as the central source to collect and disseminate ideas and information bearing on privacy procedures and policies
9. Exercising all other functions as may be necessary to accomplish its duties regarding privacy procedures and policies

In addition, the human resources staff, in carrying out its employee privacy responsibilities, should:

1. Have access to records, reports, audits, reviews, documents, papers, recommendations, or other material

2. Make investigations and reports relating to procedure and policy administration of the applicable employer facility as necessary or desirable

3. Request information or assistance as may be necessary for carrying out privacy procedure and policy responsibilities

4. Require by written notice the production of information, documents, reports, answers, records, accounts, papers, and other necessary data and documentary evidence, not otherwise restricted

5. Have direct and prompt access to the company's president or chief operating officer when necessary for the performance of privacy functions and responsibilities

6. Select, appoint, and employ the persons necessary for carrying out privacy procedures and policies

Handling Personnel Information

To limit potential employer liability for mishandling information in its collection, maintenance, use, or disclosure, the following suggestions should be considered:

1. Deal with employees truthfully.

2. Employee conduct should not be characterized as more favorable or worse than it really is.

3. Communications in and out of the workplace should be job-related and disclosed only to those who need to know.

4. In dealing with applicants, employers have a duty to find out as much job-related information as possible as part of the hiring process.

5. When asked for references, obtain or have ready a release from the former employee permitting job-related information disclosure.

6. In the absence of a release, disclose only truthful, verifiable information that falls within the former employer's business interests who is disclosing the information and the prospective employer who is seeking the information.

7. Conduct exit interviews when an employee leaves to obtain an agreement regarding how future reference inquiries should be handled.

8. To avoid liability for invasion of privacy, clearly notify employees of testing policies to remove any privacy expectation.

9. Employee adverse actions should be properly documented because this is often the employer's best litigation defense.[21]

PRIVACY COMPLAINTS

In resolving employee privacy complaints, the human resource staff should:

1. Receive and investigate complaints or information from an employee concerning violations of law, rules, or regulations along with mismanagement, gross waste of funds, abuse of authority, or a substantial and specific danger to health and safety

2. Not take, direct others to take, recommend, or approve a personnel action against any employee as a reprisal for making a complaint or disclosing information to the human resources staff, unless the complaint was made or the information disclosed with the knowledge that it was false or with willful disregard for its truth or falsity

EMPLOYEE PRIVACY COMPLAINT

The following form will help you become aware of and resolve employee privacy complaints:

[21] See Schneider, *Employers Can Protect Themselves from the Growing Number of Lawsuits Involving Personnel Information,* 154 Hum. Resources Mgmt, Ideas & Trends (CCH) 167 (Oct.16, 1987).

EMPLOYEE PRIVACY COMPLAINT

NAME _____ DATE _____

DEPARTMENT _____ TITLE _____ SUPERVISOR _____

DATE PRIVACY COMPLAINT AROSE: _____

FACTS OF COMPLAINT: _____

_____

_____

_____

_____

_____

_____

_____

_____

_____

_____

_____

HOW SHOULD THIS BE RESOLVED? _____

_____

_____

_____

_____

_____

_____

_____

_____

_____

_____

_____

SIGNED _____

EMPLOYEE DISCIPLINE AND PRIVACY

PRIVACY CONSIDERATIONS FOR EMPLOYEE DISCIPLINE

Given the increasing sympathy shown to employees by the courts, employers should act as if their disciplinary decisions are reviewable under the most restrictive standards. Even if the employer is operating in a nonunion setting, every employment action should be treated as if it were subject to labor arbitration under a collective bargaining agreement; that is, an employer should be prepared to meet a just cause standard to defend its actions.

Most collective bargaining agreements in the private and public sectors require a cause or just cause standard to sustain adverse employment actions. If this standard is not explicitly specified in a collective bargaining agreement, many arbitrators imply a just cause limitation. In the absence of precise definitions, *cause* or *just cause* may be considered any combination of:

1. The "law of the shop" regarding a particular employment action; that is the employer's response to that action developed over a given time period
2. A consistent pattern of rule and regulation enforcement, along with making these known to all employees
3. Case histories of other similar employment actions
4. Known practices of severe discipline for certain offenses because of the product manufactured, service rendered, or safety considerations
5. Offenses calling for immediate suspension and those not requiring termination
6. Workplace and outside-the-workplace offenses, along with differences in their treatment
7. General arbitral authority derived from awards, articles, and so forth
8. The arbitrator's own sense of equity and subjective judgment regarding the significance, seriousness, and weight to be given the incident, the employee's record, or the circumstances causing the employment action
9. The severity of the incident's facts
10. Attempts made to rehabilitate the employee by the employer

11. Progressive discipline steps that may or may not have been taken

12. The discipline penalty imposed as it relates to the incident's facts

13. Whether a second chance is warranted from the employee's prior record

14. Whether the employee is unreclaimable as indicated by his or her prior record or the incident's facts[22]

Before a discipline or termination decision is made, it should be reviewed by an additional management level. This may be a human resource officer or a specific employer official responsible for reviewing all proposed discipline or terminations. In the more difficult disciplinary situations, legal counsel should be consulted. The following documents should be considered:[23]

1. Performance evaluations

2. Warning notices

3. Personnel policies or work rules

4. Witness statements

5. Witness interview notes

6. Other relevant documents including complaints, written statements from the employee, other employees, accident reports, work records, overtime records, timecards, safety inspections, and so forth

After these documents are reviewed, the following should be evaluated:[24]

1. Is the employee a long-service employee?

2. Is the employee's record of promotions and salary increases inconsistent with past unsatisfactory work performance?

3. Were the employee's salary increases labeled "merit" or something else?

4. Has the employee received any commendations or awards?

---

[22] For a general discussion of cause and just cause, *see* F. Elkouri & E. Elkouri, *How Arbitration Works* 651–55 (4th ed. 1985).

[23] *See* American Hospital Association, *The Wrongful Discharge of Employees in the Health Care Industry* 52 (1987).

[24] *Id.* at 53–55.

5. Is the discipline or termination consistent with treatment given other employees in similar incidents?

6. Does the written record support the decision?

7. Does the articulated reason for the decision comply with the employer's personnel policies, work rules, and with the evidence?

8. Is there a credibility dispute and how do the employer's witnesses compare to the employee's?

9. Does the employee's explanation raise any mitigating circumstances or compelling sympathies?

10. Should an action less severe than termination be imposed?

11. Did the employer's decision maker:
    - Have firsthand knowledge of the facts?
    - Review the written record before making the decision?
    - Talk to the witnesses?
    - Present the image of a believable witness?

12. Can the employer prove the facts that allegedly exist?

13. After the discipline or termination decision has been made, it is important that:
    - The employer explain the reasons for the employer's action at an interview
    - The explanation need not be in writing, but should be candid, consistent with the evidence, and consistent with any explanation the employer intends to use
    - The interview should be carefully documented and a suitable employer witness should be present at the interview to verify the conversation

14. The reason for the discipline or termination should be discussed openly and frankly with the employee in that:
    - There should be an attempt to persuade the employee that the reason is legitimate and consistent with the employer's past practice in similar cases
    - The employee should be advised what will be told prospective employers
    - If the termination reasons are reduced to writing, they should be thorough and accurately stated
    - To avoid possible invasion of privacy, defamation, or intentional infliction of emotional distress claims, the employer should generally not disclose the reasons for the

discipline or termination to other employees or third parties

15. Centralized control of the discipline and termination process permits the employer to determine its best witness if the case is litigated:

   • This may be a member of the human resources staff who has knowledge of the relevant facts concerning the employee's work performance and the work performance of similarly situated employees

   • This should allow the employer's presentation of its case to be more coherent and easier to follow

   • A jury may be less inclined to view the litigation as a conflict between one individual against an impersonal organization with a member of the human resources staff as the employer's main witness

   • The jury might be persuaded to view the case as a test of that official's credibility and fairness as opposed to the employee's

   • If the employer does decide to have the human resources staff monitor all discipline and termination decisions, that individual should be mature, responsible, articulate, and able to convey the impression of being fair and sympathetic toward employees and their problems

EMPLOYMENT UNDERSTANDING FORM

The following form should be used at the employee's initial hiring or when a handbook is distributed, to preserve an at-will employment relationship:

EMPLOYMENT UNDERSTANDING FORM

I have received and read the ___(Employer's Name)___ handbook and understand that this handbook does not create any expressed or implied contract. It is specifically agreed and understood that my employment can be terminated by either me or the employer at any time for no reason. I understand that the Company retains the right to alter, amend, or abolish any or all of this handbook's terms at any time, for any reason and without my prior knowledge, consent, or approval.

_____

Employee Signature

_____

Date

SUPERVISOR'S RECOMMENDATION TO RETAIN
EMPLOYEE FORM

The form on the next page should be used by supervisors in evaluating whether a new hire's employment should be continued:

SUPERVISOR'S RECOMMENDATION TO
RETAIN EMPLOYEE FORM

(Employee's Name), will finish the first _____ days of employment on
_____, 19 _____. Consider the employee's work performance, attend-
ance, punctuality, and general conduct in making your recommendation:

_____   I recommend separation because:

_____

_____

_____

_____

_____

_____

_____

_____

_____

_____

_____

_____   I recommend continuing employment because:

_____

_____

_____

_____

_____

_____

_____

_____

_____

_____

_____

_____

DATED: _____   _____

                                Supervisor

DISCIPLINE NOTICE FORM

The following form should be used by employers in notifying an employee of disciplinary action:

DISCIPLINE NOTICE FORM

Employee Name: _____

Department: _____ Date: _____

   For reasons listed below, the following disciplinary action is being implemented:

Disciplinary Action: _____

Effective Date: _____ Time: _____ A.M./P.M.

Reason: _____

_____

_____

_____

_____

_____

_____

_____

Warning Against Future Misconduct: _____

_____

_____

_____

_____

_____

_____

_____

Signed: _____

Employee Receipt Acknowledgement: _____

Date of Acknowledgement: _____

2

INITIAL EMPLOYMENT CONTACTS

Initial employment contacts significantly affect employee privacy interests present in the hiring process. These privacy interests are affected whether or not hiring results. Hiring is the human resource function that develops qualified applicants and it interfaces with employee selection.

Considerable personal information must be disclosed in seeking employment. Initial employment contacts create vast information resources for immediate and subsequent employee privacy intrusions. Often the employer must verify information provided by applicants. Disclosure of employee-provided information may involve privacy interests present in beliefs, speech, associations, and lifestyles.

During initial employment contacts, the applicant must determine what and how much information should be revealed. Typically, newspaper advertisements include some job details that enable interested individuals to evaluate their qualifications. Many individuals decide not to apply after this self-analysis. Those individuals who apply generally reveal only the information necessary to obtain employment and not jeopardize their opportunities.

All information disclosed may be subject to employer verification. In verifying information, other data may be revealed that may or may not be employment-related. The additional data may be obtained with or without employee knowledge. After the employee is hired, the information may again be expanded through attendance records, compensation data, medical reviews, benefit reports, performance evaluations, disciplinary notices, and so forth.

The employer's concern is to collect information that is relevant to the evaluation of the applicant for the job to be filled.

This information may result from advertisements, applications, interviews, and hiring procedures. Procuring this employee information immediately raises privacy concerns. The employee privacy principles, procedures, and policies applicable to initial employment contacts are reviewed in this chapter.

ADVERTISEMENTS

ADVERTISEMENT PRIVACY PRINCIPLES

Newspaper advertisements in the help-wanted section are a common employer recruitment method. Some employers use advertisements to publicize their products, services, or distinctive features. Advertising may motivate applicant interest by educating readers about unique employer characteristics involving philosophy, product technology, or career opportunities.

Many applicants make their first employer contact through newspaper advertisements. Depending upon the advertisement's content, the applicant may inquire further or may refrain from making an inquiry. When someone does not apply for employment because he or she believes that it would be futile, employee privacy interests are affected by impacting speech, beliefs, association, or lifestyle. The applicant cannot properly determine whether to exercise the "right to be let alone."

Inability to exercise employee privacy interests is no different from an actual physical intrusion. These employee privacy interests may be enforced under federal and state FEP statutes or through contractual theories.

ADVERTISEMENT PROCEDURES

Preparation Considerations

Preparing an effective employment advertisement is more involved than it appears. Several preliminary considerations can ensure an advertisement's success by:

1. Checking the job description and job specifications to be sure they are correct
2. Conducting a job analysis if there is doubt about a job description's or job specification's accuracy

3. Writing the advertisement so that it can be easily read, omitting technical language
4. Selling the job to prospective applicants by writing advertisements to be appealing in structure and content, considering:
   - Printing style
   - Borders
   - Layout
   - Factual statements that highlight the job's major features[1]

Minimizing Litigation Risks

To minimize employee privacy intrusions and reduce employer litigation risks, the following should be considered:

1. Advertisements specifying sex, race, religion, age, national origin, handicap, or relating to these areas may invite employee privacy challenges under federal and state FEP statutes
2. Employers are prohibited from using help-wanted advertisements under "male" and "female" headings unless sex is a bona fide occupational qualification
3. Advertisements should be worded to avoid creating contractual commitments by not suggesting:
   - Long-term employment
   - Guaranteed job security
   - Guaranteed wages or salary
   - Career security
4. To ensure consistency, the employer should centralize responsibility for advertisement development, writing, and placement with one group, namely the human resources staff, to minimize employee privacy problems

ADVERTISEMENT POLICIES

The following employment advertisements should be considered as a guide.

---

[1] D. Myers, Human Resources Management: Principles and Practice 288–90 (1986).

Advertisement: Form 1

HAMPTON INN

- Porter
- Secretary
- Host/Hostess

Apply in person at 1800 Paper Mill Road, Wyomissing, Pennsylvania

Equal Opportunity Employer

Advertisement: Form 2

RADIOLOGY TECHS

REGISTERED AND NEW GRADS

Opportunity to work at Hazleton General Hospital. The working environment is caring, dynamic, and team-oriented.

Competitive salary and comprehensive benefits.

Interested applicants should call or write:

HUMAN RESOURCE DEPARTMENT
HAZLETON GENERAL HOSPITAL
700 E. Broad Street
Hazleton, PA 18201
(717) 545-4357

Equal Opportunity Employer

Advertisement: Form 3

MAINTENANCE MECHANIC
PIPEFITTER & PLUMBER

1st shift. $11.49/hr. Applicant must have journeyman's license.
Minimum 3–4 yrs. industrial experience.

Contact Mr. Noll at 373-4111

GLIDDEN COMPANY
3rd & Bern St.
Reading, PA 19601

Equal Opportunity Employer

Advertisement: Form 4

PERSONNEL SECRETARY

An international MONTGOMERY COUNTY based company
seeks individual to assist in Human Resources Dept. Responsibilities
will include processing medical insurance, maintenance of employee
files, Workers' Comp claims, reports, typing and clerical work plus
other independent projects.

For consideration, send your resume to:

J-28, P.O. Box 2066
Philadelphia, PA. 19103

Equal Opportunity Employer

APPLICATIONS

APPLICATION PRIVACY PRINCIPLES

The application's purpose is to elicit job-related information from an applicant to enable the employer to make an informed hiring decision. Applications affect privacy interests with respect to how much information an employer can collect regarding an applicant's personal life and experiences.

At one time, the employer could inquire into almost any area. Today, privacy constraints through federal and state FEP statutory protections apply to many traditional areas of employer inquiry involving age, marital status, pregnancy, disability, and so forth.

Privacy interests relating to permissible employer inquiries begin with the application and extend throughout, and even beyond, the employment relationship. These privacy interests do not merely limit the employment information that can be solicited, but require that, once this information is collected, the employer use it properly and protect it from unwarranted disclosures. The employer has a responsibility to make certain that employee personal matters in its records remain confidential and protected. Unauthorized employment information reading may be a privacy invasion imposing employer responsibility.

Applications generally impact employee privacy interests through federal and state FEP statutes. These privacy concerns relate to race, color, sex, national origin, handicap, and age. Inquiring into areas thate are not job-related may affect the employee's privacy by revealing beliefs, speech, associational, and lifestyle interests. Sensitive questions may pressure employee privacy expectations. The employer may obtain information that is not job-related and eliminate certain individuals from consideration based on this information. In subsequent litigation, the employer may be required to defend the use of the information requested or to explain why the information was collected but not used.

APPLICATION PREPARATION

Initially, the employer must determine what information is needed to determine which applicant is best suited for a position. This may involve inquiries into education, professional licenses or certifications, previous work experience, special skills, talents, fluency in a foreign language, and so forth. The employer's special needs for the position may warrant that certain additional information be elicited.

After determining what job-related and general background information should be collected from the applicant, the remainder of the application should be drafted to preserve applicant privacy and limit employer liability by:

1. Informing the applicant that the employment is at-will
2. Providing an applicant's acknowledgment that any information falsification or omission may result in termination
3. Requiring the applicant's representation that the information provided is complete and accurate
4. Including a release protecting the employer and those persons the employer contacts regarding references
5. Inquiring only whether the applicant has any physical condition or limitations that would disqualify him or her from performing the job; however, this may require that the applicant's physical condition be examined to determine if reasonable accommodations under federal and state FEP statutes could be made for the applicant to perform the job
6. Not inquiring regarding the applicant's filing for and/or receiving of benefits related to work-related illnesses or injuries, because this may be considered retaliation for these benefits' receipt

Application Privacy Considerations

The following should be considered regarding application privacy:[2]

1. Collecting only information that is relevant to specific employment decisions
2. Telling applicants, employees, and former employees what use will be made of the collected information
3. Letting applicants know what kinds of information will be maintained
4. Adopting reasonable procedures to ensure that application information is accurate, timely, and complete
5. Limiting application disclosure internally and externally

[2] Privacy Protection Study Commission, Personal Privacy in an Information Society app. 3 (Employment Records) (1977).

Prohibited Inquiries

Applicants are typically requested to furnish basic information involving name, address, job being applied for, experience, and education. The application form can yield information needed to compare adequately an applicant's qualifications to the job specifications. However, an improperly structured application can cause an employer problems. Employers should consider using this standard in determining whether an inquiry should be made: "How does this inquiry ensure a job-related selection?" Inquiries should not be made where they are not job-related.

Some employers ask potentially improper questions on applications involving an applicant's age, birth date, and so forth. Some application inquiries that may be difficult for employers to justify, and could encourage FEP complaints, include:

1. Arrests
2. Availability for Saturday and Sunday work
3. Bonding refusal
4. Children under 18
5. Citizenship of a country other than the United States
6. Credit record
7. Eye color
8. Garnishment record
9. Hair color
10. Height
11. Marital status
12. Number of children
13. Personal financial information
14. Sex
15. Spouse's employment status
16. Spouse's name
17. Weight

Some of this information is sought in conjunction with affirmative action reporting requirements. When that is the purpose, it is advisable to use a tear-off sheet attached to the application to minimize improper information, use, or disclosure.

APPLICATION POLICIES

The employer should prepare its application with the objectives of gathering the information necessary to make job-related hiring decisions and providing a foundation for defending against privacy-related litigation that may arise if hiring does not result or if termination subsequently occurs. Carefully drafting applications will minimize litigation exposure. The following forms should be used in developing an application that minimizes employee privacy intrusions.

Application Form 1

The following application was designed with federal and state FEP considerations in mind:

APPLICATION FORM 1 *

PLEASE PRINT

*Date: _____

Name: _____

Street: _____

City: _____

State: _____ Zip Code: _____

Area Code: _____ Business Telephone: _____

Area Code: _____ Home Telephone: _____

How were you referred? ____ Newspaper ____ School ____ On my own
                        ____ Co. Employee ____ Agency ____ Other

Name of referral source:

_____

_____

_____

_____

TYPE OF WORK DESIRED

Indicate the position for which you are applying: _____

_____

_____

What is your minimum weekly salary requirement? _____

Date available for work: _____

Do you have any commitments to another employer which might affect your employment with us? _____

_____

* This application will be considered only for employment purposes by the company for a period of ninety (90) days from this application's date after which a new application must be completed and filed.

APPLICATION FORM 1 *(Continued)*

EDUCATIONAL DATA

School	Print Name, Number and Street, City, State, and Zip Code for Each School Listing	Type of Course or Major	Graduated? (yes or no)	Degree Received
High School:				
College:				
Graduate School:				
Trade, Bus., Night, or Corres.:				
Other:				

MILITARY EXPERIENCE

Were you in U.S. Armed Forces? ____ Yes ____ No

If yes, what Branch? _____

Rank at Separation _____

Briefly describe your duties: _____

_____

APPLICATION FORM 1 *(Continued)*

EMPLOYMENT HISTORY

List present employer or most recent employer first (use other side of this application, if necessary). May we contact these employers? _____ Yes _____ No

_____

Employer: Employed   Supervisor's Name:

_____   From: _____   _____
                                              Mo./Yr.

Address:

_____   To: _____
                                              Mo./Yr.

Telephone: _____   Your Job Title

                                                                                        _____

Your Salary: Duties:

_____

_____

Start: End:

_____

Reason for Leaving: _____

_____

_____

_____

Employer: Employed   Supervisor's Name:

_____   From: _____   _____
                                              Mo./Yr.

Address:

_____   To: _____
                                              Mo./Yr.

Telephone: _____   Your Job Title:

                                                                                        _____

Your Salary: Duties:

_____

Start: End:

_____

Reason for Leaving: _____

_____

_____

_____

Employer: Employed   Supervisor's Name:

_____   From: _____   _____
                            Mo./Yr.

Address:

_____   To: _____
                            Mo./Yr.

Telephone: _____   Your Job Title:

                                             _____

Your Salary: Duties:

_____

_____

Start: End

_____

Reason for Leaving: _____

_____

_____

_____

Employer: Employed   Supervisor's Name:

_____   From: _____   _____
                            Mo./Yr.

APPLICATION FORM 1 *(Continued)*

Address:

_____   To: _____
                                    Mo./Yr.

Telephone: _____   Your Job Title:

                                                  _____

Your Salary: Duties:

_____

Start: End:

_____

Reason for Leaving: _____

_____

_____

_____

_____

GENERAL INFORMATION

Are you willing to undergo a pre-employment physical examination?
____ Yes ____ No

Have you previously applied for employment at this Company?
____ Yes ____ No
If yes, when? _____

Have you previously been employed at the Company or its subsidiaries?
____ Yes ____ No
If yes, when? _____

Are any of your relatives employed by the Company?
____ Yes ____ No

If yes, please list name and department: _____

_____

APPLICATION FORM 1 *(Continued)*

Please include any other information you think would be helpful in considering you for employment, including additional work experience, articles/books published, activities, accomplishments, and so forth. Exclude all information indicative of age, sex, race, religion, color, national origin, and handicap.

_____

_____

_____

_____

_____

_____

_____

_____

_____

_____

_____

_____

AGREEMENT

Should I be employed by the Company, I agree to conform to the Company's rules and regulations, and agree that my employment and compensation can be terminated, with or without cause, and with or without notice, at any time, at the option of either the Company or myself.

I certify that the information provided on this application is true and complete to the best of my knowledge and agree that falsified information or significant omissions may disqualify me from further consideration for employment and may be considered justification for termination if discovered at a later date.

I authorize persons, schools, current employer and previous employers, and organizations named in this application to provide the Company with any relevant information that may be required. I further release all parties providing information from any and all liability or claims for damages whatsoever that may result from this information's release, disclosure, maintenance, or use.

This application has been read by me in its entirety.

_____   _____
Signature   Date

Application Form 2

The following application was designed to solicit as little information as possible by the employer, but to place the information disclosure burden entirely on the applicant to make the choices regarding what information to reveal:

APPLICATION FORM 2

Please send one copy of this form along with a resume outlining your qualifications to ___(Employer's name and address)___ .

_____

_____

_____

_____

_____

Name: _____ Date: _____

Street: _____

City: _____ State: _____ Zip Code: _____

Current position: _____

Currently employed at: _____

How long? _____

Ultimate employment goal? _____

_____

_____

Next employment step? _____

_____

_____

Why? _____

_____

_____

Are you willing to relocate? _____

Where? _____

_____ Why? _____

_____
Signature

81

Application: Affirmative Action Information

To allow collection of certain information required by federal and state FEP statutes to meet affirmative action and other statistical information, the following information should be included on the application in an area where it can be separated from the application to avoid problematic inquiries during the hiring process:

Prior to hiring, this information may constitute sex discrimination (by revealing marital status) or national origin discrimination (by revealing an ethnic name where the person is unmarried and parents must be notified). However, this information can be obtained after hiring.

APPLICATION: AFFIRMATIVE ACTION INFORMATION

To aid in the Company's commitment to equal employment opportunity, applicants are asked to voluntarily provide the following information. This section will be separated from the application immediately upon filing.

____ Male   ____ Female

Your Age Group

1. Under 21 ____   5. 50–59 ____
2. 21–29 ____   6. 60–69 ____
3. 30–39 ____   7. 70 and over ____
4. 40–49 ____

Please check the one which best describes your race/ethnicity:

A. Mexican, Mexican-American, Chicano ____
B. Puerto Rican ____
C. Cuban ____
D. Any other Spanish/Hispanic ____

If not Hispanic, check:

E. White ____   I. Vietnamese ____
F. Black ____   J. Asian Indian ____
G. Filipino ____   K. Eskimo ____
H. American Indian ____   L. Aleut ____
   (Specify tribe)   M. Hawaiian ____
   _____   N. Samoan ____
O. Japanese ____   R. Guamanian/Chamorro ____
P. Chinese ____   X. Other, not listed _____
Q. Korean ____

Check any major disability you have a record of which may have impeded your securing, retaining, or advancing in employment:

1. Hearing ____   5. Developmental ____
2. Sight ____   6. Other disability
3. Speech ____   Specify: _____
4. Physical Orthopedic/   _____
   amputations ____   7. No disability ____

Are you a veteran, spouse of a 100% disabled veteran, or a widow or widower of a veteran?

____ Yes   ____ No

Only applicants who check "Yes" will be verified for veterans preference points in examinations which allow the addition of these points.

Application Employment Contract Disclaimer

> To preserve the at-will employment relationship, an employer should consider placing a disclaimer within the application that covers the following:

APPLICATION EMPLOYMENT CONTRACT DISCLAIMER

In consideration of my employment, I agree to conform to the Company's rules and regulations, and agree that my employment and compensation can be terminated, with or without cause, and with or without notice, at any time, at the option of either the Company or myself. I understand that no manager or representative, other than the Chief Executive Officer or (Name) , has any authority to enter into any agreement for employment for any specified time period, or to make any agreement contrary to this. Any agreement for employment for any specified time period must be in writing and signed.

_____

Signature

Application Information Release Form

To protect the employer in securing applicant references or other applicant information, the following form should be considered as part of the application:

APPLICATION INFORMATION RELEASE FORM

I authorize schools, references, prior employers, and physicians or other medical practitioners to provide my record, reason for leaving employment, and all other information they may have concerning me to the Company and I release all parties providing information from any and all liability or claims for damages whatsoever that may result from this information's release, disclosure, and use.

_____
Signature

INTERVIEWS

INTERVIEW PRIVACY PRINCIPLES

Unlike the application's written inquiry, the interview is primarily oral, although a written record may be created. After the initial interview, others may be conducted prior to the final hiring decision. At every interview, employee privacy interests may be affected, because each employer decision-making level attempts to refine the information initially requested and to determine final selection by obtaining additional information to set the applicants apart. Privacy concerns involving employee speech, beliefs, and associations may be affected by this supplementary information's collection, maintenance, use, and disclosure, along with lifestyle intrusions.

Because of federal and state FEP statutes, employers must take special care in applicant interviews. The employer may not use an applicant's race, color, sex, age, national origin, religion, marital status, or physical handicap as a basis for an employment decision, unless the employer is hiring pursuant to goals and timetables contained in its affirmative action plan. Similarly, an interviewer may not ask an applicant impermissible questions related to these areas, nor may a former employer be asked these questions during a written or telephone reference check.

Minimizing Litigation Risks

To maximize the benefits that can be derived from interviews, and to prevent statements during an interview that may lead to liability, the employer should use:[3]

1. Well-informed and well-prepared interviewers who:
    *   Become well-informed sufficiently prior to the interview by reviewing applications, resumes, and other pertinent information
    *   Know what further job-related information should be obtained from the applicant during the interview
    *   Know what information to convey about the employer

---

[3] *See* American Hospital Association, The Wrongful Discharge of Employees in the Health Care Industry 20–21 (1987).

- Know what information to convey about the particular job for which the applicant has applied

2. Interviewers who are not only knowledgeable about the employer's advantages and benefits, but are aware that certain statements should not be made to "sell" applicants on the employer involving:

- Overemphasizing the employer's virtues to avoid creating enforceable employee rights against the employer if the employee is later terminated

- Becoming specific and promising definite employment terms and conditions greater than or different from the employer's oral or written policies, to avoid binding commitments

- Asking questions that could be considered discriminatory or an employee privacy intrusion; that is, only job-related inquiries should be used

INTERVIEW INQUIRY POLICY

The following interview policy is intended to acquaint interviewers with what questions can and cannot be asked to protect employee privacy interests and minimize employer liability for improper information collection, maintenance, use, or disclosure:

INTERVIEW INQUIRY POLICY

Instructions to Interviewers: The following are examples of impermissible interview inquiries and their acceptable counterparts:

<table>
<tr><td>Unacceptable</td><td>Acceptable</td></tr>
</table>

Age

Unacceptable	Acceptable
1. What is your age?	1. Statement that hire is subject to verification that applicant meets legal age requirements
2. When were you born?	
3. Dates of attendance or completion of elementary or high school	2. If hired can you show proof of age?
	3. Are you over eighteen years of age?
	4. If under eighteen, can you, after employment, submit a work permit?

Arrest, Criminal Record

Unacceptable	Acceptable
1. Arrest record	1. Have you ever been convicted of a felony, or, within two years, a misdemeanor which resulted in imprisonment? This question should be accompanied by a statement that a conviction will not necessarily disqualify the applicant from the job requested
2. Have you ever been arrested?	

Birthplace, Citizenship

Unacceptable	Acceptable
1. Birthplace of applicant, applicant's spouse, or relatives	1. Can you, prior to employment, submit verification of your legal right to work in the United States?
2. Are you a U.S. citizen?	2. Statement that this proof may be required after employment
	3. Requirements that applicant produce naturalization, first papers, or alien card prior to employment

Bonding

Unacceptable	Acceptable
1. Questions regarding refusal or cancellation of bonding	1. Statement that bonding is a condition of hire based on the position

Military Service

1. General questions regarding military service that pertain to date, type of discharge, and so forth
2. Questions regarding service in a foreign military

1. Questions regarding relevant skills acquired during applicant's United States military service

Name

1. Maiden name

1. Have you ever used another name?
2. Is any additional information regarding a name change, assumed name use, or nickname necessary to check on your work or education record? If yes, please explain

National Origin

1. Questions regarding nationality, lineage, ancestry, national origin, descent, or parentageof applicant, applicant's parents, or spouse
2. What is your mother tongue?
3. Language commonly used by applicant
4. How applicant acquired ability to read, write, or speak a foreign language

1. Language applicant reads, speaks, or writes for job-related purposes

Notice in Case of Emergency

1. Name and address of relative to be notified in case of accident or emergency

1. Name and address of person to be notified in case of accident or emergency

Organizations/Activities

1. List all organizations, clubs, societies, and lodges to which you belong.

1. List job-related organizations, clubs, professional societies, or other associations to which you belong. Omit those indicating or referring to your race, religious creed, color, national origin, ancestry, sex, or age

Physical Condition/Handicap

1. Questions regarding applicant's general condition, state of health, or illness
2. Questions regarding receipt of worker's compensation
3. Do you have any physical disabilities or handicaps?

1. Statement by employer that offer may be made contingent on applicant passing a job-related physical examination
2. Do you have any physical condition or handicap that may limit your ability to perform the job requested? If yes, what can be done to accommodate your limitation?

Race, Color

1. Questions regarding applicant's race or color
2. Questions regarding applicant's complexion or color of skin, eyes, or hair
3. Requirement that applicant affix a photograph to application
4. Requesting applicant, at his or her option, to submit a photograph
5. Requiring a photograph after interview but before employment

1. Statement that photograph may be required after employment

References

1. Questions of applicant's former employers or acquaintances which elicit information specifying the applicant's race, color, religious creed, national origin, ancestry, physical handicap, medical condition, marital status, age, or sex

1. By whom were you referred for a position?
2. Names of persons willing to provide professional and/or character references for the applicant

Religion

1. Questions regarding applicant's religion
2. Religious days observed
3. Does your religion prevent you from working weekends or holidays?

1. Statement by employer of regular days, hours, or shifts to be worked

1. Questions indicating applicant's sex
2. Questions indicating applicant's marital status
3. Number and/or ages of children or dependents
4. Questions regarding pregnancy, childbearing, or birth control
5. Name(s) of spouse or children of applicant
6. Questions regarding child care

1. Name and address of parent or guardian if applicant is a minor
2. Statement of employer policy regarding work assignment of related employees
3. Do you have any relatives already employed? If so, give names and positions held

HIRING PROCEDURE

Hiring Privacy Principles

To protect employee privacy interests and limit employer liability, an overall hiring procedure should be developed that considers advertisements, applications, and interviews. The overall hiring procedure should ensure that only relevant or job-related information necessary for employment decisions is collected, maintained, and used. Likewise, this information's sensitivity should be preserved through confidentiality procedures in effect prior to, during, and after employment termination. This should be done to minimize employee privacy claims that may arise out of federal or state FEP statutory violations as well as those arising from other legal complications.

Hiring Procedure

General Considerations

In developing an overall hiring procedure, the following should be considered in preserving employee privacy interests:

1. Determine who should be the interviewer
2. Determine who should review records
3. Obtain information from verifiable sources
4. Obtain information by acceptable methods
5. Obtain information only from reliable consumer reporting agencies and regularly reevaluate the selection
6. Maintain information confidentiality
7. Exercise caution in reference checking
8. Inform applicants what information will be maintained
9. Inform applicants of the uses to be made of collected information
10. Adopt procedures to assure the information's accuracy, timeliness, and completeness
11. Permit review, copying, correction, or amendment of this information
12. Limit internal use

13. Limit external disclosures, including disclosures made without authorization, to specific inquiries or requests to verify information

14. Provide for a regular internal compliance review of hiring procedures

Minimizing Litigation Risks

Due to litigation's high cost and the at-will employment doctrine's changing character, employers should attempt to structure their hiring procedures and policies to minimize their legal risk by:[4]

1. Ensuring that interviewers do not make improper or exaggerated promises

2. Examining personnel policies, handbooks, and manuals to make certain that they contain no promises the employer is unable or unwilling to keep, by removing any language that might imply that employment is other than at-will by:
   - Avoiding terms like "permanent employee"
   - Changing "probationary period" to "initial review period"
   - Considering including in each employee handbook a statement:

     That "These policies are subject to unilateral change without notice"

     or:

     Preserving the at-will nature of the employment relationship by disclaiming the creation of any employment contract
   - If the publication contains work rules or a list of termination causes, it should state that the rules/list is not all inclusive

3. Having every applicant sign a written acknowledgment that any employment with the employer is at-will. This acknowledgment should be:
   - Included as part of the actual application
   - A statement that the application has been read in its entirety

---

[4] *See* id. at 13–84.

Hiring Policies

Checklist before Employment

This form should be used as a record to ensure that the employer's procedures and policies are adequately explained to employees, in order to obtain a consistent understanding and enforcement:

CHECKLIST BEFORE EMPLOYMENT

The Company asks that you complete the following checklist before reporting for employment. It is important that the Company orient you to its procedures and policies. By signing in the appropriate place, you are acknowledging that the corresponding topic has been fully explained and that any questions you may have have been answered to your satisfaction.

TOPIC	EMPLOYEE SIGNATURE
1. Employment date.	_____
2. Rate of pay/compensation.	_____
3. I understand I may be requested to perform various unrelated tasks from time to time.	_____
4. I understand that my supervisor will introduce me to my fellow employees and personnel in other departments I may have contact with at various times.	_____
5. I have answered all questions accurately and completely on my Employee's State Withholding (W4) Allowance Certificate.	_____
6. I have answered all questions accurately and completely on my IRS Employee's Withholding (Federal W-4) Allowance Certificate.	_____
7. I have answered all questions accurately and completely on my Employment Eligibility Verification (Form I-9).	_____
8. I have completed my Employee Information Sheet.	_____
9. I have received and read a copy of the Employee Handbook—Book number _____.	_____
10. I have received and read a copy of the Group Insurance Benefits Booklet. I also received and completed an enrollment card for these benefits.	_____
11. I have received and read a copy of the Company-paid, weekly income insurance plan.	_____
12. I have received and read a copy of the plan summary for the profit-sharing program and understand when I am eligible to participate and the benefits I can derive through participation in the plan.	_____

_____

Date

_____

Employee Signature

_____

Supervisor Signature

Hiring Policy

An overall employer hiring policy is shown on pp. 97–99.

HIRING POLICY

Section 1. Purpose. It is the Company's policy always to hire a qualified employee. This selection will be based on qualifications, skill, training, personality, and ambition displayed by the applicant. It is the Company's commitment to comply with this hiring policy.

Job openings not filled from within will be filled by referrals, walk-ins, or advertisement respondents. Active files for applicants are maintained by the Human Resources Department for six (6) months. These may be used and should be reviewed when seeking new employees. The Plant Manager or Manager requesting additional employees should submit in writing a request identifying the job, position, and need to the Human Resources Department.

Section 2. General Procedures. Prior to employing an individual, certain preliminary steps must be taken to ensure uniformity of personnel practices and compliance with federal and state employment statutes. The following procedures are to be used:

a. Applicant reception;
b. Preliminary interview and screening by the Human Resources Department;
c. Application completion;
d. Testing;
e. Interview with the prospective supervisor;
f. Reference checks;
g. Preliminary selection by the Human Resources Department after consultation with the prospective supervisor;
h. Final selection by the Plant Manager, supervisor, and Human Resources Department; and
i. Applicant hiring.

Section 3. Reception. The applicant will be met in the Human Resources Department's lobby where literature and information concerning the Company will be made available. All referred applicants, walk-ins, or advertisement respondents report to this area first. It is the Company's policy to treat each of these applicants with the same consideration as a customer. All applicants, whether hired or not, can spread good will for the Company or give it a bad name, based on the treatment they receive. The Company's policy is to maintain a good image for attracting qualified applicants.

Section 4. Preliminary Interview and Screening by the Human Resources Department. A short preliminary interview by the Human Resources Department's staff will be held with the applicant to identify the most promising applicants and those who are not qualified.

Section 5. Application. After the preliminary interview, all applicants are given an application to complete. The questions used on this application are in compliance with federal and state FEP statutes and regulations. The application also includes clauses covering falsification of records and an agreement to submit to medical testing, which are also signed by the applicant. The applicant is also asked at this time for information under the Immigration Reform and Control Act (IRCA) of 1986. If the applicant cannot comply with this Act, he or she will not be considered for employment. Once obtained, IRCA information will be kept separate from the application.

Section 6. Testing. All applicants who are approved as possible candidates, whether they are referred by employees, walk-ins, or advertisement respondents, will not be tested until job requests are given to the Human Resources Department. An outside agency will do the testing to ensure that the Company adheres to federal and state FEP statutes which require that the overall selection process show no evidence of adverse impact on minority groups.

Section 7. Interview with Prospective Supervisor. If the applicant's testing proves positive, an interview with the prospective supervisor takes place. The times for the interviews are set up to be mutually convenient for both the supervisor and the applicant. This interview is set up to: (a) assess the applicant; (b) describe the job and working conditions to the applicant by touring the area in which he or she would work; and (c) create goodwill for the Company, whether or not the applicant is hired. To accomplish these objectives, the supervisor must be alert, perceptive, able to keep accurate records, free from prejudice, and even-tempered. Supervisors must also avoid any questioning or conduct that violates federal and state FEP statutes. After the interview, the applicant will be told that he or she will be contacted by the Human Resources Department. The supervisor does not offer the job to the employee. A checklist will be given to the supervisor to make sure that certain points are covered during the interview. The supervisor will return the application with the completed interview checklist to the Human Resources Department for determination as to whether to continue the hiring procedure.

Section 8. Reference Checking. If the interview proves positive, the Human Resources Department will check references with former employers, schools attended, and so forth. The applicant must sign a consent form to be sent to certain employers who might not otherwise be willing to forward information on the applicant.

Section 9. Preliminary Selection by the Human Resources Department after Consultation with Prospective Supervisor. A preliminary selection will be made by the Human Resources Department and the supervisor after they are satisfied that qualified applicants are available. If no qualified applicants are available, other applicants will be sought.

Section 10. Final Selection by the Plant Manager, Prospective Supervisor, and the Human Resources Department. A final selection will be made by the Plant Manager, the prospective supervisor, and the Human Resources Department after all are satisfied that a qualified selection is available. All must agree on wages, terms, and conditions for the new employee. A checklist will be used to cover these points and all will sign this Selection Form.

Section 11. Placement—Hiring of Applicant. The Human Resources Department will contact the selected applicant and offer employment. Details of the wages, terms, and employment conditions will be discussed. If the applicant accepts, the Human Resources Department will set up a time for the employee to sign in and begin the Company's orientation program.

Section 12. Rejected Applicants. In most circumstances, a number of applicants will be interviewed for a particular position. It is conceivable that at times more than one applicant will progress through the interview procedure, but only one will be chosen. If other applicants would have been eligible for the position, these approved applicants will be retained in a special referral file for up to six (6) months to be considered for additional openings that might occur either in the same department or in other departments or shifts. As openings develop, these applicants will be referred to supervisors for consideration, along with additional new applicants, as required by the supervisor to make a quality selection.

Section 13. Applicability. Anyone being hired as a full-time employee is subject to this hiring procedure. Employees hired on a temporary basis through outside temporary services are subject to this hiring policy.

3

EMPLOYEE DATA VERIFICATION

After an application is submitted, employers use various procedures to verify employee information. Data verification may occur with or without the individual's consent or knowledge. This affects employee privacy interests present in speech, beliefs, and associations by the collection, maintenance, use, and disclosure of information other than that which the employee voluntarily revealed.

Verification is the selection method that checks applicant information accuracy. Almost every qualification an applicant offers for employment consideration can be verified. Verification sources include previous employers, schools, colleges, military records, certifying or licensing bodies, public records, and so forth. Public records include those from courts, law enforcement agencies, licensing bureaus, tax assessors, and financial departments.

Some verification sources are more accurate than others. Verifying a college degree can be accomplished by contacting the college registrar, while a driver's license can be checked with the state driver's license department. However, it is sometimes more difficult to obtain accurate information from previous employers. Employers may be more cooperative when the information request is accompanied by an applicant-signed release.

Information accuracy can be substantially increased by informing applicants that the information they furnish will have a direct bearing upon their hiring. Also, applicants should be instructed that the information they furnish will be carefully verified. These procedures greatly decrease the inconsistency between information furnished by applicants and that obtained through verification.

Some companies provide employers with services that include verifying job experience, work performance, attendance, training, education, criminal convictions, motor vehicle driving records, military records, and so forth. These companies also conduct applicant background searches and provide comprehensive reports by reviewing workers' compensation claims, credit bureau records, bankruptcy filings, and interviews with coworkers and neighbors to determine an applicant's reputation regarding honesty, alcohol, drug abuse, and so forth.

Verification information may be irrelevant and not job-related. To safeguard employee privacy interests and minimize employer litigation exposure, procedures and policies must be developed to counteract these privacy problems. This chapter reviews employee privacy interests relevant to employment data verification that are inherent in credit checks, arrest records, criminal convictions, fingerprints, photographs, immigration requirements, reference checks, and skill testing.

CREDIT CHECKS

CREDIT CHECK PRIVACY PRINCIPLES

Credit information collection, maintenance, use, and disclosure present significant employee privacy concerns by potentially revealing nonjob-related data affecting speech, beliefs, and associational interests. This information may be used by employers in evaluating applicants and/or employees for hiring, promotion, reassignment, or retention. Sometimes credit information is obtained for nonjob-related purposes; personal finances are generally not relevant to the job applied for or held.

Federal and state statutes place certain restrictions on credit information used for employment purposes. Nonjob-related credit reports may violate federal and state FEP statutes. A requirement that applicants and employees have a good credit record may have to be justified by a legitimate job-related business necessity.

CREDIT CHECK PROCEDURES

To ensure that employee privacy interests are observed in undertaking a credit check, an employer should:[1]

---

[1] *See* Privacy Protection Study Commission, Personal Privacy in an Information Society 250–51 (1977).

1. Select a reputable credit agency and periodically review the choice
2. Notify the applicant and/or employee that a credit check will be performed and indicate:
   - The types of information expected to be collected that are not collected on the application, and, as to information regarding character, general reputation, and mode of living, each area of inquiry
   - The techniques that may be used to collect the information
   - The sources that are expected to provide the information
   - The parties to whom and circumstances under which information about the individual may be disclosed without authorization and the information that may be disclosed
   - The statutory procedure by which the individual may gain access to any resulting record
   - The procedures the individual may use to correct, amend, or dispute any collected record
   - That information in any report prepared by a consumer reporting agency may be retained by that organization and subsequently disclosed by it to others
3. Obtain the applicant's and/or employee's written consent for undertaking a credit check
4. Not share the information received regarding an applicant and/or employee with potential creditors
5. Limit credit checks to job-related information and purposes
6. Consider credit information highly confidential and sensitive
7. Certify that credit information will only be used for job-related purposes

CREDIT CHECK POLICIES

Credit Check Policy

The following policy should be considered regarding credit information collection, maintenance, use, and disclosure:

CREDIT CHECK POLICY

Section 1. Definitions. For the purposes of this policy, the following terms shall mean:

a. *Consumer report.* Any report containing information relating to an individual's credit record or manner of obtaining credit directly from a creditor of the individual or from a consumer reporting agency; and also shall include information pertaining to an individual's character, general reputation, personal characteristics, or mode of living obtained through personal interviews with neighbors, friends, or associates of the individual reported on, or others with whom he or she is acquainted or may have knowledge concerning any of these information items.

b. *Consumer reporting agency.* Any person who, for monetary fees or dues, regularly engages in assembling or evaluating employment information to be used regarding individuals.

c. *Employment purposes.* A report used by the Company for evaluating an individual for employment, promotion, reassignment, retention, and so forth.

d. *Individual.* A person who has applied for employment or who is currently employed by the Company.

Section 2. Procurement. The Company shall request a consumer report only for legitimate employment purposes, which must be job-related.

Section 3. Written Permission. The Company shall procure a consumer report only after written permission from the individual has been received.

Section 4. Information Inspection. The Company shall, upon request and proper identification of any individual, allow the inspection of any and all consumer reports maintained regarding that individual.

Section 5. Confidentiality. The Company shall maintain all consumer report information in strict confidence and shall not disclose it absent the individual's written permission.

Credit Check Consent Form

The following should be used to safeguard the employer's interest in requesting credit-related information from an applicant or employee:

CREDIT CHECK CONSENT FORM

Based on the requirements of the job for which I am applying, I authorize __(Company's Name)__ to conduct a job-related credit check.

_____   _____
Date   Applicant/Employee's Name

ARREST RECORDS

ARREST RECORD PRIVACY PRINCIPLES

Many employers believe that arrest history is critical, or at least relevant, to employment. Arrest information raises employee privacy concerns because it indicates only that a law enforcement agency believed that probable cause to arrest existed for some offense. It does not reflect guilt, nor that the person actually committed the offense.

Refusing employment or terminating employees because of arrest records is not permitted without evidence that it is job-related to the employer's business. Even when a legitimate pre-employment inquiry is made regarding arrest records, an applicant's rejection based solely on an arrest record may violate federal and state FEP statutes.

ARREST RECORD PROCEDURES

The following should be considered regarding arrest records and their possible employment use:

1. That a differentiation be made between arrest and conviction
2. That a careful evaluation be made of the frequency and severity of arrests
3. Age at time of the arrest
4. The elapsed time since an arrest
5. The whole individual: that is, his or her aptitudes, abilities, interests, and educational level, rather than one aspect of personal history
6. The job's nature and its relation to the employability of those with arrest records
7. Geographic location of the incidents involved

ARREST RECORD POLICIES

The following policy should be considered regarding arrest record collection, maintenance, use, and disclosure:

ARREST RECORD POLICY

Section 1. Conviction. A "conviction" shall include a plea, verdict, or finding of guilt, regardless of whether sentence is imposed by a court.

Section 2. Collection. The Company shall not ask an applicant or employee to disclose, through any written form or verbally, information concerning an arrest or detention that did not result in conviction or information concerning a referral to and participation in any pretrial or posttrial diversion program.

Section 3. Use. The Company shall not seek from any source or utilize as a factor in determining any employment condition including hiring, promotion, termination, apprenticeship, or any other training program leading to employment, any record of arrest or detention that did not result in conviction or any record regarding a referral to and participation in any pretrial or posttrial diversion program.

Section 4. Exception. The Company may ask an applicant or employee about an arrest for which the applicant or employee is out on bail or on his or her own recognizance pending trial.

CRIMINAL CONVICTIONS

CRIMINAL CONVICTION PRIVACY PRINCIPLES

Criminal convictions present different employee privacy concerns than do arrests. A conviction is a societal judgment regarding an individual's actions. Unlike arrests, a conviction record is complete. Guilt and accountability have been finalized.

Uneasiness exists for employee privacy regarding conviction information collection, maintenance, use, and disclosure. Even though an employer may take legitimate employment actions based on criminal convictions when it correlates the offense's nature, gravity, and time elapsed since the conviction to job-relatedness, privacy concerns remain over subsequent use and disclosure that impact associational and lifestyle interests. Conviction record use may violate federal and state FEP statutes.

CRIMINAL CONVICTION PROCEDURES

Employers must consider a conviction's legitimate job-related circumstances regarding impact and effect before determining that employment would be inconsistent with safe and efficient business operation. These circumstances include:

1. The job and its responsibilities
2. The time, nature, and number of convictions
3. Each conviction's facts
4. Each conviction's job-relatedness
5. The length of time between a conviction and the employment decision
6. Employment history before and after the conviction
7. Rehabilitation efforts
8. Whether the particular conviction would prevent job performance in an acceptable businesslike manner
9. Age at the time of the conviction
10. The conviction's geographic location

The following policy should be considered regarding conviction record collection, maintenance, use, and disclosure:

CRIMINAL CONVICTION POLICY

Section 1. Conviction. A "conviction" shall include a plea, verdict, or finding of guilt, regardless of whether sentence is imposed by a court.

Section 2. Conviction's Use. The Company may consider any conviction as a possible justification for the refusal, suspension, revocation, or termination of employment when it directly relates:

a. To the applicant's possible performance in the job applied for; or
b. To the employee's possible performance in the job which the employee holds.

Section 3. Conviction's Job-Relatedness. In determining whether a conviction is job-related, the Company will consider, among other things:

a. The job and its responsibilities;
b. The time, nature, and number of convictions;
c. Each conviction's facts;
d. Each conviction's job-relatedness;
e. The length of time between a conviction and the employment decision;
f. Employment history before and after the conviction;
g. Rehabilitation efforts;
h. Whether the particular conviction would prevent job performance in an acceptable businesslike manner;
i. Age at the time of the conviction; and
j. The conviction's geographic location.

Section 4. Excluded Convictions. The Company will not consider:

a. Convictions which have been annulled or expunged;
b. Convictions of a penal offense for which no jail sentence may be imposed; or
c. Conviction of a misdemeanor in which the period of twenty years has elapsed since the conviction's date and during which there has been no subsequent arrest or conviction.

FINGERPRINTS

FINGERPRINT PRIVACY PRINCIPLES

Fingerprinting has generally been considered a valid employer collection method related more to verifying information than to compulsory incriminating fact extraction. Despite its primary use in verifying information, some states regulate fingerprinting in order to limit employee privacy abuses. Statutes may prohibit an employer from requiring that an applicant or employee be fingerprinted for the purpose of furnishing information to a third party, as a condition precedent to securing or retaining employment, where this information could be used to the applicant's or employee's detriment.

FINGERPRINT PROCEDURES

Should fingerprints be used, they should only be considered:

1. To verify employee identity, where this is in doubt, or for receipt of an employee benefit
2. For meeting immigration requirements

FINGERPRINT POLICY

The following policy should be considered regarding fingerprint collection, maintenance, use, and disclosure:

FINGERPRINT POLICY

The Company shall not require, as a condition to securing or retaining employment, that an applicant or employee be fingerprinted where fingerprints could be used to the applicant's or employee's detriment in a non-job-related situation.

PHOTOGRAPHS

PHOTOGRAPH PRIVACY PRINCIPLES

Photographing employees during the initial hiring process raises privacy objections, because race, color, national origin, sex, and age may be unnecessarily revealed for non-job-related use. These privacy interests have been protected primarily under federal and state FEP statutes. However, employers have been permitted to photograph employees at the workplace when a legitimate job-related business purpose existed. Legitimate employee photographing may be used to improve safety, for example, or to identify employees who are violating employer rules.

PHOTOGRAPH PROCEDURES

To ensure that employee privacy interests are considered, an employer should:

1. Not require photographs on applications or at interviews
2. Use photographs only for legitimate business purposes; that is, for job performance monitoring
3. Obtain employee consent when photographs are used in employer literature or advertisements

PHOTOGRAPH POLICIES

Photograph Policy and Consent

The policy should be considered regarding photograph collection, maintenance, use, and disclosure.

A consent to use employee photographs should be executed at hiring and may take the form shown on page 112.

PHOTOGRAPH POLICY

The Company shall not require, as a condition to securing or retaining employment, that an applicant or employee be photographed where photographs could be used to the applicant's or employee's detriment in a non-job-related manner.

PHOTOGRAPH CONSENT

The Company may use my name, picture, or likeness for any advertising, publicity, or other legitimate business purpose, regardless of whether I am employed by the Company when the name, picture, or likeness is used. This consent is given in consideration of my employment. The legitimate use of my name, picture, or likeness will not result in an invasion of privacy, defamation, intentional infliction of emotional distress, or a violation of any other property right that I may have. I understand that I will receive no additional consideration, compensation, or benefit if my name, picture, or likeness is used. Any negatives, prints, or other material for printing or reproduction in connection with the use of my name, picture, or likeness will be the Company's property.

_____   _____
Date   Employee

_____
Witness

IMMIGRATION REQUIREMENTS

IMMIGRATION PRIVACY PRINCIPLES

The Immigration Reform and Control Act of 1986 (IRCA) creates an additional recordkeeping requirement for employers in an attempt to curtail illegal immigration into the United States. It requires every employer to ask applicants for specific written verification establishing that they can be employed. Civil and criminal penalties may be imposed on employers who knowingly hire or recruit an alien.

IRCA prohibits employers from discriminating against applicants on the basis of their national origin. It is an unfair immigration-related employment practice to discriminate against any individual in hiring, recruitment, or termination because of that individual's national origin or citizenship status.

The potential for employee privacy problems exists in the collection of age, national origin, or other potentially discriminatory data required by IRCA. To minimize employee privacy intrusions by not obtaining sensitive applicant data, the required IRCA information should not be collected until the applicant pool has been sufficiently narrowed prior to hiring. Once collected, it should be maintained separate from the employee's personnel file, to prevent disclosures that could have a discriminatory impact. This will minimize employee privacy challenges arising out of federal or state FEP statutes.

IMMIGRATION PROCEDURES

Guidelines for Completing the Employment Eligibility Verification Form (Form I-9)

The following are guidelines for completing Form I-9[2] (Employment Eligibility Verification Form).

Verifying Employment Eligibility. The Immigration Reform and Control Act of 1986 (IRCA) requires employers to hire only citizens and aliens who are authorized to work in the United States. The Employment Eligibility Verification Form (Form I-9) has been developed for verifying that persons are eligible to work. IRCA requires an employer to:

---

[2] Adapted from the Handbook for Employers, Immigration and Naturalization Service (June 1987).

1. Have all employees complete Form I-9 when they begin working
2. Check documents establishing employee identity and eligibility to work
3. Properly complete Form I-9
4. Retain Form I-9 for at least three years
5. Retain Form I-9 until one year after the person leaves employment, if the person is employed for more than three years
6. Present Form I-9 for inspection to an Immigration and Naturalization Service (INS) or Department of Labor (DOL) officer upon request

Unlawful Discrimination.   If the employer has four or more employees, the employer may not discriminate against any individual other than an unauthorized alien in hiring, terminating, recruiting, or referring for a fee because of that individual's national origin or, in the case of a citizen or intending citizen, because of his or her citizenship status.

The Civil Rights Act of 1964 (Title VII) and the remedies against discrimination it provides are applicable. Title VII prohibits discrimination against any individual on the basis of national origin in hiring, termination, assignment, compensation, and other employment terms and conditions. National origin discrimination claims against employers with 15 or more employees should be filed with the Equal Employment Opportunity Commission (EEOC).

Under IRCA, national origin discrimination charges against employers with 4 through 14 employees, and citizenship discrimination charges against employers with 4 or more employees, should be filed with the Office of Special Counsel in the Department of Justice. Discrimination charges may be filed either by the person who believes that he or she was discriminated against in employment on the basis of national origin or citizenship status, by a person on their behalf, or by INS officers who have reason to believe that discrimination has occurred. Discrimination charges must be filed within 180 days of the discriminatory act. The Office of Special Counsel will notify the employer by certified mail within 10 days upon receipt of a discrimination charge. After investigating the charge, the Special Counsel may file a complaint with an administrative law judge. If the Special Counsel does not file a complaint within 120 days of receiving the charge, the person making the charge (other than an INS officer) may initiate the filing of a complaint with an administrative law judge. The administrative law judge will conduct a hearing and issue a decision.

Employers found to have engaged in discriminatory practices will be ordered to cease the prohibited practice. They may also be:

1. Ordered to hire, with or without back pay, individuals directly injured by the discrimination
2. Pay a fine of up to $1,000 for each individual discriminated against, or up to $2,000 for each individual in cases of employers previously fined
3. Keep certain records regarding applicant and employee hiring

Should a court decide that the losing party's claim has no reasonable basis in fact or law, the court may award attorneys' fees to prevailing parties other than the United States.

Penalties for Prohibited Practices. If an investigation reveals that an employer has violated IRCA regarding employees hired after November 6, 1986, INS may take action. When INS intends to impose penalties, it will first issue a Notice of Intent to Fine. Employers who receive a notice may request a hearing before an administrative law judge. If a hearing is not requested within 30 days, the penalty will be imposed.

Violations of IRCA include civil penalties for:

1. *Hiring or continuing to employ unauthorized employees.* Employers determined to have knowingly hired unauthorized employees or to be continuing to employ persons knowing that they are or have become unauthorized may be fined as follows:
   - First violation of not less than $250 and not more than $2,000 for each unauthorized employee
   - Second violation of not less than $2,000 and not more than $5,000 for each unauthorized employee
   - Subsequent violations of not less than $3,000 and not more than $10,000 for each unauthorized employee
2. *Failing to comply with recordkeeping requirements.* Employers who fail properly to complete, retain, and present for inspection the Form I-9 as required by law may be fined as follows:

- Civil fines of not less than $100 and no more than $1,000 for each employee for whom the form was not completed, retained, or presented
- In determining penalties, consideration shall be given to the business's size, good faith efforts to comply, the seriousness of the violation, and whether the violation involved unauthorized employees

3. *Requiring indemnification.* Employers found to have required a bond or indemnity from an individual against liability may be fined $1,000 and ordered to make restitution, either to the person who was required to pay the indemnity, or, if that person cannot be located, to the United States Treasury

4. *Recruiting unauthorized seasonal agricultural workers outside the United States.* Employers who knowingly recruit unauthorized workers outside the United States to perform seasonal agricultural labor may face the same penalties as for hiring unauthorized workers, unless the workers recruited have been granted Special Agricultural Worker (SAW) status

Criminal penalties for violation of IRCA include:

1. *Engaging in a pattern or practice of knowingly hiring or continuing to employ unauthorized employees.* Employers convicted for having engaged in a pattern or practice of knowingly hiring unauthorized aliens after November 6, 1986, may be fined as follows:
   - Fines of up to $3,000 per employee and/or six months imprisonment
   - The same penalties apply to engaging in a pattern or practice of recruiting unauthorized seasonal agricultural workers outside the United States
   - Criminal sanctions will be reserved for serious or repeated violations

2. *Engaging in fraud, false statements, or otherwise misusing visas, immigration permits, and identity documents.* Persons who use fraudulent identification or employment eligibility documents or documents that were lawfully issued to another, or who make a false statement or attestation for purposes of satisfying the employment eligibility requirements may be imprisoned for up to five years, or fined, or both

Timetable for Employer Verification Requirements.

1. *December 1, 1986 through May 31, 1987 (Public education period):*
   - The initial period established by IRCA for publication of regulations and dissemination of forms and information
   - During this period, citations were not issued and fines were not levied

2. *June 1, 1987 through May 31, 1988 (Citation period):*
   - The one-year period for public education, voluntary compliance, and initial enforcement
   - INS worked with employer associations, labor unions, and others to provide assistance, develop voluntary co-operation
   - Penalties were not imposed for first-offense violations during this period.
   - A warning citation was issued explaining the violation
   - For subsequent or repeated violations, civil or criminal penalties could be imposed

3. *June 1, 1987 through September 1, 1987 (Special rule period):*
   - Employers were permitted to hire or to continue to employ employees who attest on the Form I-9 that they have applied or intend to apply for: legalization, Special Agricultural Worker, and/or Cuban/Haitian status
   - This could occur even if the workers have not yet received work authorization documents from the INS

4. *June 1, 1988 (Effective date for full enforcement):*
   - As of this date, citations were no longer be issued for first violations
   - Employers who violate IRCA may face civil or criminal penalties

5. *June 1, 1987 through November 30, 1988 (Deferred period for employers of seasonal agricultural workers):*
   - Penalties did not apply to employers of seasonal agricultural workers during this period
   - The deferral did not apply to the prohibition against recruitment of unauthorized employees who are outside the United States
   - As of December 1, 1988, INS began full enforcement of IRCA regarding agricultural employers

Persons for Whom Form I-9 Must Be Completed.

1. For persons hired after May 31, 1987, a Form I-9 must be completed:
    *   Within three business days of the date of the hire
    *   If the person is employed for less than three days, the employer must complete Form I-9 before the end of the employee's first working day
2. For persons hired between November 7, 1986 and May 31, 1987, Form I-9 must have been completed before September 1, 1987

Employers need not complete Form I-9 for:

1. Persons hired before November 7, 1986
2. Persons hired after November 6, 1986, who left employment before June 1, 1987
3. Persons employed for domestic work in a private home on an intermittent or sporadic basis
4. Persons who provide labor and are employed by a contractor providing contract services such as employee leasing
5. Persons who are independent contractors

How to Complete Form I-9. Form I-9 contains two sections. The employee completes the first section containing Steps 1, 2, and 3. If a preparer or translator assists the employee, the preparer or translator completes Step 4. The second section, containing Steps 5 and 6, should be completed by the employer.

When completing Form I-9, the employee will need to provide a document or documents that establish identity and employment eligibility. Some documents establish both identity and employment eligibility. These documents appear in List A on the bottom half of the Form I-9. Other documents establish identity alone (List B) or employment eligibility alone (List C). If the person does not provide a document from List A, he or she must produce one from List B and one from List C.

The employer should review the document or documents provided by the person. Documents should appear to be genuine and relate to the individual.

If employees cannot complete Section 1 by themselves or need the form translated, someone may assist them. The preparer or translator should read the form to the employee, help with Step 1 and Step 2 as needed, have the employee sign or mark the form, and follow Step 4.

If a minor under age 16 cannot produce a List A document or one of the identity documents on List B, he or she is exempt from producing one if:

1. A parent or legal guardian completes Section 1 and writes in the space for the minor's signature the words, "minor under age 16"

2. The parent or legal guardian completes the "Preparer/ Translator Certification"

3. The employer writes in Section 2 the words, "minor under age 16" under List B in the space after the words, "Document Identification #"

If this procedure is followed, the minor must still produce a List C document showing employment eligibility.

Instructions for Recruiters and Referrers for a Fee. IRCA's provisions also apply to those who recruit persons and refer them to potential employers in return for a fee, and to those who refer or provide documents or information about persons to employers in return for a fee. The provisions do not apply to persons who recruit for their own company or business. Union hiring halls that refer union members or nonunion individuals who pay membership dues are not considered to be recruiters or referrers for a fee.

Recruiters and referrers for a fee are not required to verify the status of persons referred between November 6, 1986 and May 31, 1987. Starting June 1, 1987, they should complete Form I-9 when a person they refer to an employer is hired by that employer. The form should be completed within three business days of the hire.

Recruiters and referrers may designate agents to complete the verification procedures on their behalf, including national associations or employers. If the employer who hires the referred individual is designated as the agent, the employer need only provide the recruiter or referrer with a Form I-9 photocopy. Recruiters or referrers who designate someone to complete the verification procedures on their behalf are still responsible for compliance with IRCA, and may be found liable for violations.

Recruiters and referrers must retain the Form I-9 for three years after the date the referred individual was hired by the employer. They must also present forms for inspection to an INS or DOL officer after three days' advance notice. The penalties also apply to recruiting and referring unauthorized employees for a fee (on or after June 1, 1987).

Applicable Documents for Verifying Employment Eligibility. Certain documents have been designated for determining IRCA employment eligibility. (The employee must provide a document or documents that establish identity and employment eligibility.)

Some documents establish both identity and employment eligibility. These are listed on the Form I-9 under List A, "Documents that Establish Identity and Employment Eligibility." If a person does not provide a document from List A, he or she must provide one document that establishes identity and one document that establishes employment eligibility.

To establish identity, the person must provide a document in List B. To establish employment eligibility, one of the immigration documents in List C must be furnished.

If an employee is unable to provide the required document or documents within three days, he or she must at least produce, within three days, a receipt showing that he or she has applied for the document. The employee must produce the document itself within 21 days of hiring.

LIST A

Documents that Establish Identity and Employment Eligibility

1. United States Passport
2. Certificate of United States Citizenship (INS Form N-560 or N-561)
3. Certificate of Naturalization (INS Form N-550 or N-570)
4. Unexpired foreign passport which:
   - Contains an unexpired stamp reading "Processed for I-551. Temporary Evidence of Lawful Admission for permanent residence. Valid until _____. Employment authorized"; or
   - Has attached to it a Form I-94 bearing the same name as the passport and containing an employment authorization stamp, so long as the period of endorsement has not yet expired and the proposed employment is not in

conflict with any restrictions or limitations identified
on the Form I-94

5. Alien Registration Receipt Card (INS Form I-151) or Resident Alien Card (INS Form I-551), provided that it contains a photograph of the bearer

6. Temporary Resident Card (INS Form I-688)

7. Employment Authorization Card (INS Form I-688A)

LIST B

Documents that Establish Identity

For individuals 16 years of age or older:

1. State-issued driver's license or state-issued identification card containing a photograph or, if the driver's license or identification card does not contain a photograph, identifying information should be included listing name, date of birth, sex, height, color of eyes, and address

2. School identification card with a photograph

3. Voter's registration card

4. United States military card or draft record

5. Identification card issued by federal, state, or local government agencies

6. Military dependent's identification card

7. Native American tribal documents

8. United States Coast Guard Merchant Mariner Card

9. Driver's license issued by a Canadian government authority

For individuals under age 16 who are unable to produce one of the documents listed above:

1. School record or report card

2. Clinic doctor or hospital record

3. Daycare or nursery school record

LIST C

Documents that Establish Employment Eligibility

1. Social Security number card, other than one which has printed on its face "not valid for employment purposes,"

that must be a card issued by the Social Security Administration; a facsimile such as a metal or plastic reproduction that people can purchase is not acceptable

2. An original or certified copy of a birth certificate issued by a state, county, or municipal authority bearing an official seal
3. Unexpired INS employment authorization
4. Unexpired reentry permit (INS Form I-327)
5. Unexpired Refugee Travel Document (INS Form I-571)
6. Certification of Birth issued by the Department of State (Form FS-545)
7. Certification of Birth Abroad issued by the Department of State (Form DS-1350)
8. United States Citizen Identification Card (INS Form I-197)
9. Native American tribal document
10. Identification Card for use of Resident Citizen in the United States (INS Form I-179)

Counterfeit Document Detection

In determining the legitimacy of documents presented for Immigration Reform and Control Act verification, employers should:

1. Be aware of the document's information
2. Determine whether the information pertains to the individual presenting the document: i.e., if the person appears to be 18 and the identification says 45, there is a problem; if a man presents an identification with a woman's picture, there is also a problem
3. Look for alterations of an official document through erasures, photograph substitutions, and so forth; official documents are never altered but are replaced
4. Check to be sure the document is squarely cut
5. Ascertain that printing and engraving is parallel with the document's edges, along with being sharp, clear, and unbroken
6. View documents as suspect where printing and engraving is dull, unclear, broken, or blurred
7. Not deny employment to someone based on a suspect document, but should contact the local INS office for verification of the document's number

8. Check with the state employment agency to determine if it has a certification process to verify an applicant's documents through the INS and issue a letter of certification to potential employers, with the certification letter serving as eligibility proof

IMMIGRATION POLICIES

Immigration Policy

The following policy should be considered in complying with the Immigration Reform and Control Act of 1986:

UNLAWFUL IMMIGRATION DISCRIMINATION

The Company will not discriminate against any individual other than an unauthorized alien in hiring, disciplining, terminating, recruiting, and so forth because of that individual's national origin or, in the case of a citizen or intending citizen, because of his or her citizenship status.

REFERENCE CHECKS

REFERENCE CHECK PRIVACY PRINCIPLES

Reference checks affect employee privacy interests by disclosing speech, belief, association, and lifestyle interests that are not job-related. This information is frequently collected or disclosed absent the employee's knowledge. It often involves former employers who may be solicited without the employee's knowledge or consent.

Reference checks represent another employer effort to compile and verify the most complete and accurate information regarding applicants. From the former employer's perspective, detailed reference requests present a litigation risk against the former employer by the former employee. Many employers limit their reference request response to verifying the former employee's employment dates, job title, and salary. However, requesting detailed references from former employers is one precaution an employer can take during the hiring process to limit its vulnerability to employment litigation.

Some states statutorily regulate employee references. Federal or state FEP statutes, along with claims for invasion of privacy and defamation, may also offer employee protection.

A defense to a defamation claim is that a former employer has a qualified privilege to communicate in good faith when responding to an inquiry by one with a legitimate information interest. The former employer has the burden of establishing good faith and that the recipient had a legitimate information interest.

By failing to request references, the employer may risk negligent hiring liability. Negligent hiring arises out of employee acts committed while in the employer's service but outside the employee's employment scope. While an employer generally is not liable for employee acts outside of the employment's scope, employer liability for negligent hiring has been found where an employee was responsible for others' safety or security.

REFERENCE CHECK PROCEDURES

Reference Check Methods

Proper reference checking is time-consuming. It demands personal involvement and extends beyond having someone make telephone calls to references listed on an application. Possible approaches to reference-checking include:

1. Meeting with the applicant's references because:
   - People are much more willing to be open in person
   - It provides the opportunity to interpret facial expressions and body language which may, in addition to words, indicate how the reference actually feels about the applicant's prior work performance
2. Using the telephone
3. Checking references by mail

Providing References

In providing references, the following should be considered:

1. Review the legal aspects concerning what information can be disclosed absent an employee's consent
2. Check that the human resources staff has distributed procedures and policies regarding information disclosure:
   - Content
   - Circumstances
   - Eligible persons
3. Ensure that the information's accuracy is substantiated by factual records
4. Communicate the procedure and policy regarding references
5. Instruct all personnel that they are not to discuss another employee's performance with those outside the company

Reference Checking

In checking references, the following should be considered:

1. Obtain the employee's written permission to check references
2. Check references before making the final job offer
3. If a discrepancy exists between facts or recommendations, a more extensive investigation should be undertaken
4. Be skeptical of all subjective evaluations, especially those that do not include verifiable acts or behavior

5. View silence as an indication for further investigation; an
    employer may attempt to avoid wrongful termination liti-
    gation by negotiating a settlement with an employee that
    includes no unfavorable references

REFERENCE CHECK POLICIES

Reference Checking Policy

The following policy should be used in collecting, maintaining,
using, and disclosing references:

REFERENCE CHECKING POLICY

Absent an employee or a former employee's written consent, the Company
will not provide information, except name, job title, and employment dates, regarding its current or former employees unless required by federal or state law
or court order. All employee information requests must be referred to the Human Resources Department. Supervisors or other employees are not permitted
to respond to a reference request. Telephone inquiries will not be answered.
Only written inquiries from the person seeking the information on that person's letterhead with name and title will be considered.

INFORMATION RELEASE FORM

The following form should be used by employers when requesting references on behalf of applicants or employees:

INFORMATION RELEASE FORM

I, __(Name)__, hereby authorize the Company to release the following information regarding my employment with the Company to __(Company's Name, Person, etc.)__ :

Information List

_____

_____

_____

_____

_____

_____

_____

_____

_____

_____

_____

_____

_____

_____

_____

_____

Date: _____   _____

                                        Signed

SKILL TESTING

SKILL-TESTING PRIVACY PRINCIPLES

For employers, a desire exists to fill jobs with employees qualified for the work assigned. This desire, combined with only a vague knowledge of what the law exacts as prerequisites for skill testing, presents important employee privacy considerations.

It has generally been held that skill testing offers an objective standard by which to predict job performance. Some tests, however, eliminate ethnic minorities from certain positions by favoring education levels typical of a white, middle-class background. Performance by the economically disadvantaged on such tests has been poor.

Educational and industrial psychologists have played a major role in developing tests that attempt to predict job performance. These tests remove some of the subjectivity used in employee selection. Employment testing has developed into a highly sophisticated and technical field with its own language, its own standards, and its own complex methodology.

Test is a generic word encompassing a systematic method of measuring applicant qualifications through pencil and paper instruments, oral questions, the performance of exercises, or the manipulation of objects. Tests may be commercially prepared or custom-constructed by an employer or consultant. Tests can be grouped into the following categories:[3]

1. *Achievement test,* which measures the extent of a person's knowledge or competence within a field
2. *Aptitude test,* which measures innate or acquired capacities to learn an occupation
3. *Interest inventory,* which, while nominally a test, is more a self-assessment of interests that either correlate to those of individuals who are successfully employed in a particular occupation or can otherwise be used to determine an individual's suitability for a particular job
4. *Manual dexterity or motor test,* which measures a number of motor functions, including reaction time, quickness of arm movements, multilimb coordination, and finger dexterity
5. *Mental ability test,* which measures the ability to reason,

[3] *See* D. Myers, Human Resources Management: Principles and Practice 359–64 (1986).

perceive relationships, understand numerical properties, and solve quantitative problems

6. *Performance test*, which measures demonstrated performance, usually on a piece of equipment

7. *Sensory test*, which measures hearing and vision, including color vision

8. *Situational test*, which is a generic term for a variety of exercises that measure an applicant's responses to workplace situations

9. *Competitive group exercise*, which assigns roles to applicants, who receive various instructions concerning how the role should be played

10. *In-basket test*, which evaluates applicants' abilities to handle a work basket of events representative of those encountered on the job they are seeking

11. *Computer game*, which measures the ability of applicants to evaluate information, usually quantitative data, plan responses, and make decisions

12. *Work sample*, which measures an applicant's performance on an important job task representative of what could actually occur on the job

13. *Role playing (RP)*, which is typically two persons playing assigned roles; however, RP differs from group exercises with assigned roles because only two people are involved. It is used to test for applicant knowledge, training, skills, and abilities in handling employee performance appraisal interviews, evaluating employee ideas, assisting employees in receiving help for personal problems, and resolving disciplinary problems

14. *Assessment center (AC)*, a selection method in which participants engage in multiple exercises, some of which are simulations, and their performance is appraised by pooled assessments of trained assessors

For employee privacy, testing can have a significant impact on information collection, maintenance, use, and disclosure. Depending upon the test, it may reveal privacy interests present in employee speech, beliefs, information, association, and lifestyle. These privacy concerns are essentially protected by federal and state FEP statutes.

FEP statutes generally require that a protected classification not be a factor in employment selection. If a selection procedure has a disproportionate impact that excludes protected persons, its use is unlawful unless the procedure is demonstrably a reasonable job performance measure; i.e., unless it is job-related or justified by business necessity.

Under the Civil Rights Act of 1964 (Title VII), the Uniform Guidelines on Employee Selection Procedures have been developed. The Guidelines define a *selection procedure* broadly as any measure, combination of measures, or procedure used as a basis for an employment decision, including hiring, promotion, membership, referral, retention, selection, training, or transfer. Selection procedures include traditional paper and pencil tests, performance tests, training programs, probationary periods, informal or casual interviews, unscored application forms, and physical, educational, and work experience requirements.

Title VII does not prohibit employers from giving or acting on the results of a professionally developed ability test where the test, its administration, and action on it are not designed, intended, or used to discriminate. However, a professionally developed test must be job-related.

SKILL TESTING PROCEDURES

Skill Testing Use Determinations

In determining whether testing should be used, the following should be considered:

1. A determination of the selection objective: a given position, occupation, program, career, and so forth
2. A determination of basic selection standards: what skills and knowledge are necessary
3. Labor market, for determining whether qualified applicants are available for testing
4. Cost utility: whether the testing can be done economically without becoming extremely costly

Skill Testing Safeguards

Employers must be aware of the possible employee privacy challenges that may arise from testing. They must review their internal testing procedures and policies along with the necessity for the test's job-related use. Failure to do this may result in costly litigation and exposure to damages if an employer is challenged. To safeguard employee privacy interests in testing, the employer should:

1. Not over rely on tests
2. Use other screening methods, including interviews, background verifications, and reference checks, along with tests
3. Use test results as added information, not to terminate an employee
4. Contact the test's developer to recheck the test if someone receives an extremely poor score but has good recommendations, job performance, and so forth
5. Use tests at the end of the hiring process when applicants have been narrowed to the best choices
6. Maintain test score confidentiality
7. Ensure that the test is job-related and does not measure extraneous non-job-related factors

SKILL TESTING POLICY

The following policy should be considered in collecting, maintaining, using, and disclosing test information:

TESTING POLICY

Section 1. Testing Procedures. In addition to written, oral, and performance tests, the Company may authorize an evaluation of education and experience, medical tests, physical strength and physical agility tests, and other types of tests, singly or in combination as job-related circumstances warrant. For promotional tests, the Company may authorize other performance criteria involving seniority and performance evaluations developed under a uniform system.

Section 2. Test Scheduling. The Company shall give due consideration to the convenience of the applicants, consistent with its needs, in determining dates, times, and locations of tests.

Section 3. Security.

a. The Company will establish appropriate procedures to ensure that all applicants for a test are given equal opportunity to demonstrate their qualifications in that:

   (i) The Company will establish proper precautions to prevent an unauthorized person from securing in advance questions or other materials to be used in a test, unless the questions or materials are available to all applicants; and

   (ii) When the conditions under which a test is held have materially impaired its competitive nature or worth in assessing qualifications, the Company will order that the tests or appropriate sections thereof, if severable, be cancelled. New tests or parts of tests may be substituted, if possible.

b. The Company will establish appropriate procedures to ensure that the identity of the applicants in all tests does not adversely affect the objective rating or scoring of test papers.

c. The Company will disqualify an applicant who impersonates another or has another person impersonate himself or herself in connection with a test, or who uses or attempts to use unauthorized aids or assistance, including copying or attempting to copy from or helping or attempting to help another applicant in any part of a test, or who otherwise seeks to attain undue advantage in connection with the test.

d. No applicant in a test shall copy, record, or transcribe any test question or answer, or remove from the testing room any question sheet, answer sheet, booklet, scrap papers, notes, or other papers or materials related to the test's content. Applicants shall be notified of this action and no examiner, proctor, monitor, or other person charged with the supervision of an applicant or group of applicants shall have authority to waive it. The Company may disqualify a candidate or refuse to certify an eligible person who violates this section.

Section 4. Preservation of Test Records. The Company shall ensure that the following documents are maintained as official records:

a. The test's original copy;
b. The test's description;
c. The test's instructions;
d. The scoring keys or other scoring standards used;
e. The examiners' reports; and
f. The resulting eligible list.

Section 5. Test Paper Inspection.

a. The Company will, upon request of an applicant, authorize the applicant to inspect his or her test documents in the presence of an authorized Company official. The inspection shall not include authorization to copy test instructions, questions, or answers, and will be conducted to maintain security of the testing program.

b. The Company may authorize review of the application and test papers of an applicant, upon request and for official purposes, by law enforcement or other public officials where there are legitimate inspection reasons. Copies of test materials will not be made available except as provided by applicable statutes or regulations.

c. The Company will authorize the disclosure of applications and test papers to a private individual only where the individual seeking access can demonstrate a clear necessity to pursue a legitimate legal right. The Company will take necessary precautions to avoid disclosure of the identities of the persons whose applications and test papers are being examined. Where it is evident that the information release would operate to prejudice or impair a person's reputation or personal security, access to the information shall be denied.

Section 6. Information Regarding Unsuccessful Applicants. Except as provided in Section 5 (Test Paper Inspection), the test papers of applicants who failed all or part of a test or who voluntarily withdrew from the test shall not be exhibited or disclosed nor shall information be released concerning their test participation.

4

WORKPLACE RECORDS

Considerable employment information is collected, maintained, used, and disclosed by employers. This information is used to hire, discipline, terminate, place, transfer, promote, demote, train, compensate, and provide full or partial fringe benefits. Information may be collected, maintained, used, or disclosed without employee notice, knowledge, or consent.

Employment record privacy and integrity is important for both employees and employers, in that nonjob-related information may be collected, maintained, or used. These records, usually referred to as *personnel files*, generally contain the employee's personal, employment, and medical history. *Personal history* concerns prior background and work history. *Employment history* details current work history regarding wages, promotions, disciplinary actions, commendations, sick days, vacation days, positions held, and performance evaluations. *Medical history* contains information about the employee's physical and psychological health. This chapter reviews policies and procedures relevant to employment records involving personal and medical information.

EMPLOYMENT RECORDS

EMPLOYMENT RECORD PRIVACY PRINCIPLES

Employer methods for collecting, maintaining, accessing, using, and disclosing employment information vary. Certain employment record aspects are regulated by federal and state statutes. These statutes generally set forth what employment information may be collected, along with providing for employee access and the right to review and copy record contents. Some statutes permit employees to place a counterstatement in the record when information is incorrect or challenged.

Various states require employers to permit employees to inspect their personnel records. This includes records that have been used to determine employment qualifications, promotion, compensation, or disciplinary action up to and including termination. The employer is required to maintain the personnel files at the place the employee reports to work or to make them available there upon reasonable notice.

Some statutes require that certain employment information be maintained by employers. Employee record privacy is thus affected, because employers, despite legal restrictions, may use detailed application blanks, interviews, and similar questionable information collection devices involving polygraph examinations, honesty tests, credit checks, and so forth.

In providing employment information, the employee relinquishes control of sensitive personal information, along with the opportunity to verify the accuracy of information that may be developed from these disclosures. Collecting inaccurate employment information is possible because each employer has its own recordkeeping system.

Employers frequently receive requests for employment information from other employers, social workers, insurance companies, credit bureaus, government officials, and union business agents. The employee initially revealed this information to obtain employment or to maintain it. Disclosure may occur for a purpose unrelated to employment that is against the employee's best interest. Through these disclosures, the employee again loses control of sensitive personal information as well as the opportunity to verify the information's accuracy. Dependence upon the employer's good will or personal values creates problems over what *confidentiality* means for employment records.

Employment records may result in privacy claims arising out of invasion of privacy, defamation, intentional infliction of emotional distress, negligent maintenance or disclosure of employment records, fraudulent misrepresentation, and public policies. A state constitutional privacy right may protect personnel files from disclosure to third parties. Employee requests to review personnel files of co-employees may violate the co-employee's right guaranteed by a state constitution. The employer, as the private information's custodian, cannot waive employee privacy rights that are constitutionally guaranteed this protection.

Contractual litigation theories are also applicable to employment record privacy interests. Privacy interests may receive protection in employment contracts, restrictive covenants, employment handbooks and policies, and collective bargaining agreements.

EMPLOYMENT RECORD PROCEDURES

General Considerations

Overall considerations for preparing employment record privacy procedures and policies should include:

1. A uniform system of collecting, maintaining, accessing, using, and disclosing employment information
2. Preserving and protecting employee privacy confidentiality
3. Collecting employment information by reviewing:[1]
   - The number and types of records maintained
   - Information items
   - Information uses made within the employer's decision-making and nondecision-making structure
   - Information disclosure made to those other than the employer
   - The extent to which employees are aware and regularly informed of the uses and disclosures that are made of this information
4. Fair information collection procedures and policies concerning applicants, employees, and former employees that:[2]
   - Limit information collection to that which is job-related
   - Inform what records will be maintained
   - Inform of the uses to be made of this information
   - Adopt procedures to assure information accuracy, timeliness, and completeness
   - Permit review, copying, correction, or information amendment
   - Limit internal use
   - Limit external disclosures, including disclosures made without authorization, to specific inquiries or requests to verify information
   - Provide for a regular policy compliance review
   - Contain an employment application with a waiver authorizing the employer to disclose employee file contents to those to whom the employee grants access; that is, reference checks by subsequent employers, and to make a credit check where applicable

---

[1] *See* Privacy Protection Study Commission, Pesonal Privacy in an Information Society 235 (1977).

[2] *Id*. at 237–38.

- Indicate on the file when and where these employee reviews took place
- Restrict information access to those with a need to know and those who are authorized outside of the employer; that is law enforcement officials, government agencies, and so forth
- Ensure that information retention conforms to applicable law
- Contain a privacy clause

Employment Record Inspection Procedures

An employee's right to inspect his or her personnel file, however, is not absolute. Statutes may not grant an employee a right to inspect any records relating to an investigation of a possible criminal offense or to reference letters maintained by the employer. The employer is entitled to impose reasonable restrictions upon an employee's access to his or her personnel file. These may take various forms, including:[3]

1. Requiring the employee to submit a written request to inspect his or her personnel file
2. Allowing inspection only by appointment
3. Allowing inspection only during regular business hours
4. Allowing inspection only on the employee's own time
5. Allowing inspection only in the presence of an employer representative
6. Limiting inspection frequency
7. Allowing employees to copy or obtain copies of their own personnel files
8. Permitting employee amendment of this information
9. Documenting inspection dates by employee

Employment Record Retention

Certain federal statutes require that employers collect, maintain, and disclose various forms of employment information.[4] Among these are the following.

---

[3] *Id.* app. 3 at 35–43.

[4] For an exhaustive list of other federal statutes and their requirements, *see* Policy and Practice Series (BNA) (1989).

Civil Rights Act of 1964 (Title VII)

Records to Be Retained	Time Period
A. Any personnel or employment record made or kept by an employer, including applications and records having to do with hiring, promotion, demotion, transfer, layoff, termination, pay rates, compensation terms, and selection for training or apprenticeship	A. Six months from the date of making the record or taking the personnel action involved, whichever occurs later
B. Personnel records relevant to a discrimination charge or action brought by the Attorney General against the employer, including records relating to the charging party and to all other employees holding similar positions, applications or test papers completed by an unsuccessful applicant and by all other candidates for the same position	B. Until final disposition of the charge or action
C. For apprenticeship programs:	C. Retained for:
1. A chronological list of names and addresses of all applicants, dates of application, sex, and minority group, or file of written applications containing the same information; and other records pertaining to apprenticeship applicants, including test papers, interview records, and so forth	1. Two years or the period of the successful applicant's apprenticeship, whichever is later
2. Any other record made solely for completing report EEO-2 or similar reports	2. One year from due date of the report
D. Employers with 100 or more employees must file a copy of EEO-1—Employer Information Report	D. Current report must be retained indefinitely; six months

Age Discrimination in Employment Act (ADEA)

Records to Be Retained	Time Period
A. Payroll records containing each employee's name, address, date of birth, occupation, rate of pay, and compensation earned per week	A. Three years
B. Personnel records relating to: 1. Job applications, resumes, or other replies to job advertisements, including applications for temporary positions and records pertaining to failure or refusal to hire 2. Promotion, demotion, transfer, selection for training, layoff, recall, or termination 3. Job orders submitted to an employment agency or union 4. Test papers in connection with employer-administered aptitude or other employment tests 5. Physical examination results considered in connection with a personnel action 6. Job advertisements or notices to the public or employees regarding openings, programs, or opportunities for overtime work	B. One year from the date of the personnel action to which the record relates, except 90 days for applications and other applicant pre-employment records for temporary jobs
C. Employee benefit plans, written seniority or merit rating systems	C. Period plan or system is in effect plus one year
D. Personnel records, including the above, relevant to an action commenced againstthe employer	D. Until final disposition of the enforcement action

Vocational Rehabilitation Act of 1973

Records to Be Retained	Time Period
(Federal contractors/subcontractors)	
A. For handicapped applicants and employees, complete and accurate employment records required by the Act. The Department of Labor suggests that this requirement may be met by annotating the application or personnel form of the handicapped applicant or employee to indicate each vacancy, promotion, and training program for which he or she was considered, including a statement of reasons for any rejection that compares the handicapped individual's qualification to those of the person selected, as well as any accommodations considered. Descriptions of accommodations actually undertaken also should be attached	A. One year
B. Records regarding complaints and actions taken under the Act	B. One year

Executive Order No. 11246 (Affirmative Action)
(September 24, 1965, as amended)

Records to Be Retained	Time Period
(Federal contractors, subcontractors)	Not specified
Written affirmative action programs and supporting documentation, including required utilization analysis and evaluation; other records and documents relating to compliance with applicable EEO nondiscrimination and affirmative action requirements, including records and documents on nature and use of tests, test validations, and test results as required; and compliance with construction industry EEO plans and requirements	
A. Log & Summary of Occupational Injuries and Illnesses, briefly describing recordable causes of injury and illness, extent and outcome of each incident, and summary totals for calendar year (Effective January 1, 1983, the following industries are exempt: retail trade, finance, insurance and real estate, and services)	A. Five years following the end of the year to which they relate
B. Supplementary Record, containing more detailed information for each occurrence of injury or illness	B. Five years following the end of the year to which they relate
C. Complete and accurate records of all medical examinations required by the law	C. Duration of employment plus 30 years, unless a specific OSHA standard provides a different time period
D. Records of any personal or environmental monitoring of exposure to hazardous materials	D. 30 years

Immigration Reform and Control Act of 1986

Records to Be Retained	Time Period
Form I-9, Employment Eligibility Verification, must be completed by all employers for all new employees hired after November 7, 1986. This form must be completed within three days after hiring	Must be retained for three years after the employee's hiring or for one year after employment termination, whichever is later

Employment Record Confidentiality

Regarding confidentiality, it should initially be ascertained whether the employee has a reasonable privacy expectation in the employment information. When this reasonable privacy expectation exists, information should not be released absent employee consent or authorization. In evaluating disclosure interests, the following should be considered:

1. The request's originator
2. The request's purpose
3. The relationship between the employee and employer regarding any third party requesting this information
4. Restricting disclosure to job-related information
5. Information accuracy
6. A privacy interest in not releasing the information
7. A statutory or other duty requiring or not requiring information disclosure

EMPLOYMENT RECORD POLICIES

Employment Records: Basic Policy

The following should be considered a basic policy for employment record collection, maintenance, use, and disclosure:

EMPLOYMENT RECORDS POLICY

Section 1.   Employee.   Any person currently employed or subject to recall after layoff or leave of absence with a right to return to a position with the Company or a former employee who has terminated services within the preceding year.

Section 2.   Open Records.   The Company shall, upon an employee's request, which the Company may require to be in writing, permit the employee to inspect any personnel documents which are, have been, or are intended to be used in determining that employee's qualifications for employment, promotion, transfer, additional compensation, termination, or other disciplinary action, except as provided in Section 9 (Exceptions). The inspection right encompasses personnel documents in the possession of a person, corporation, partnership, or other association having a contractual agreement with the Company to keep or supply a personnel record. An employee may request all or any part of his or her records, except as provided in Section 9 (Exceptions). The Company shall grant at least two inspection requests by an employee in a calendar year when requests are made at reasonable intervals, unless otherwise provided in a collective bargaining agreement. The Company shall provide the employee with the inspection opportunity within seven working days after the employee makes the request or, if the Company can reasonably show that the deadline cannot be met, the Company shall have an additional seven working days to comply. The inspection shall take place at a location reasonably near the employee's place of employment and during normal working hours. The Company may allow the inspection to take place at a time other than working hours or at a place other than where the records are maintained if that time or place would be more convenient for the employee. Nothing in this policy shall be construed as a requirement that an employee be permitted to remove any personnel records or any part of these records from the place on the Company's premises where the records are made available for inspection. The Company retains the right to protect its records from loss, damage, or alteration to ensure the integrity of its records. If an employee demonstrates that he or she is unable to review his or her personnel record at the employing unit, the Company may, upon the employee's written request, mail a copy of the requested record to the employee.

Section 3.   Copies.   The employee may obtain a copy of the information or part of the information contained in the employee's personnel record. The Company may charge a fee for providing a copy of the information. The fee shall be limited to the actual cost of duplicating the information.

Section 4.   Personnel Record Inspection by Designated Representatives.   An employee who is involved in a current grievance against the Company may designate in writing a representative of the employee's union, collective bargaining unit, or other representative to inspect the employee's personnel record which may have a bearing on the grievance's resolution, except as provided in Section 9 (Exceptions). The Company shall allow the designated representative to inspect that employee's personnel record in the same manner as provided under Section 2 (Open Records).

Section 5. Personnel Record Correction. If the employee disagrees with any information contained in the personnel record, a removal or correction of that information may be mutually agreed upon by the Company and the employee. If an agreement cannot be reached, the employee may submit a written statement explaining the employee's position. The Company shall attach the employee's statement to the disputed portion of the personnel record. The employee's statement shall be included whenever that disputed portion of the personnel record is released to a third party as long as the disputed record is a part of the file. The inclusion of any written statement attached in the record, without further comment or action by the Company, shall not imply or create any presumption of Company agreement with its contents.

Section 6. Disclosure of Disciplinary Action: Written Notice.

a. The Company shall not disclose a disciplinary report, letter of reprimand, or other disciplinary action to a third party, to a party who is not a part of the Company's organization, or to a party who is not a part of a labor organization representing the employee, without written notice as provided in this section.

b. The written notice to the employee shall be by first-class mail to the employee's last known address and shall be mailed on or before the day the information is disclosed.

c. This section shall not apply if:
   (i) The employee has specifically waived written notice as part of a written, signed employment application with another employer;
   (ii) The disclosure is ordered to a party in legal action or arbitration; or
   (iii) Information is requested by a government agency as a result of a claim or complaint by an employee, or as a result of a criminal investigation by the agency.

Section 7. Review of Record Prior to Release of Information. The Company shall review a personnel record before releasing information to a third party and, except when the release is ordered to a party in a legal action or arbitration, delete disciplinary reports, letters of reprimand, or other records of disciplinary action which are more than four years old.

Section 8. Record of Nonemployment Activities. The Company shall not gather or keep a record of an employee's association, political activities, publications, communications, or nonemployment activities, unless the employee submits the information in writing or authorizes the Company in writing to keep or gather the information. This prohibition shall not apply to the activities that occur on the Company's premises or during the employee's working hours which interfere with the performance of the employee's legitimate job duties or the duties of other employees or activities, regardless of when and where occurring, which constitute criminal conduct or may reasonably be expected to harm the Company's property, operations, business, or could by the employee's action cause the Company financial liability. A record which is kept by the Company as permitted under this section shall be part of the personnel record.

Section 9. Exceptions. The right of the employee or the employee's designated representative to inspect his or her personnel records does not apply to:

a. Reference letters for that employee;
b. Any portion of a test document, except that the employee may see a cumulative total test score for either a section of or the entire test document;
c. Materials used by the Company for management planning, including but not limited to judgments, external peer review documents or recommendations concerning future salary increases and other wage treatments, management bonus plans, promotions, and job assignments, or other comments or ratings used for the Company's planning purposes;
d. Information of a personal nature about a person other than the employee if disclosure of the information would constitute a clearly unwarranted invasion of the other person's privacy;
e. Records relevant to any other pending claim between the Company and employee which may be discovered in a judicial proceeding; and
f. Investigatory or security records maintained by the Company to investigate criminal conduct by an employee or other activity by the employee which could reasonably be expected to harm the Company's property, operations, or business or could by the employee's activity cause the Company financial liability, unless and until the Company takes adverse personnel action based on information in the records.

Section 10. Administration. The Director of Human Resources or an authorized representative shall administer and enforce the provisions of this policy.

Section 11. Complaints. If an employee alleges that he or she has been denied his or her rights under this policy, he or she may file a complaint with the Human Resources Department. The Human Resources Department shall investigate the complaint. The Human Resources Department shall attempt to resolve the complaint by conference, conciliation, or persuasion.

Employment Records: Comprehensive Policy

The following should be considered as a comprehensive employment record policy for use by employers in collecting, maintaining, using, and disclosing employee information:

EMPLOYMENT RECORDS POLICY

Section 1. Purpose. To establish policies and procedures for the collection, maintenance, access, use, and disclosure of employee information.

Section 2. Objectives. To provide a uniform system of collecting, maintaining, accessing, using, and disclosing employee information, along with preserving and protecting the personal privacy of all wage and salaried employees.

Section 3. Personnel Records.

a. An employment record is to be established for each employee upon hiring.
b. Official employment records for current employees are to be maintained by the Human Resources Department.
c. Documents maintained in official employment records are classified permanent or temporary, as defined in Sections 4 (Record Access) and 6 (Type of Information Kept). Permanent information will always remain in the official employment record when an employee transfers or terminates. Temporary information is to be retained for four years, unless otherwise indicated,and then is to be removed in accordance with Section 7 (Request for Information).
d. The following information is specifically prohibited from being placed in official employment records:
    (i)   Arrest records, upon acquittal or when formal charges have been dropped;
    (ii)   Investigative material regarding a civil, criminal, or administrative investigation of alleged wrongdoing by an employee which resulted in the employee's acquittal;
    (iii) National identification;
    (iv)   Racial identification, except data used in support of the Company's affirmative action program;
    (v)   Ethnic information;
    (vi)   Political affiliation;
    (vii) Religious affiliation;
    (viii) Written criticisms of which an employee is not aware; and
    (ix)   Financial disclosure information.

Section 4. Record Access.

a. Official employment records are to be secured in locked file cabinets during nonwork hours. Operating instructions for computer terminals are to be accessible only to persons designated by the Human Resources Department to operate the terminals and are to be secured during nonwork hours.
b. Only the Human Resources Department and its designees are to have access to official employment records, to data maintained on the computer system file, and to computer-produced reports.
c. The following are to have access to all information in official employment records and to information on the computer system when needed in the performance of their duties, provided that requests for access are made to the Human Resources Department:

    (i)   President;

    (ii)   Division head and designees;

    (iii)   Affirmative action officer;

    (iv)   An employee's department director;

    (v)   An employee's immediate supervisor and those in direct chain of command above the immediate supervisor; and

    (vi)   The Human Resources Department.

d. Employees and persons with written permission of employees have the right to review official employment records and reference files. Reviews must be conducted in the presence of the Human Resources Department at times amenable to both, and an employee may have a representative present. Employees may request copies of documents in their employment records; however, they are not permitted to alter, remove, add, or replace any documents. The Human Resources Department may charge reasonable fees when requested to provide copies of all materials contained in the official employment record or when frequent requests for copies of materials are received from the same employee.

e. Employees have a right to submit rebuttals to any material in their official employment records. Rebuttals are to be acknowledged by the Human Resources Department. Rebuttals and acknowledgments shall become part of the official employment record in the same permanent or temporary category as the material being rebutted. If rebuttals are submitted by inactive employees, the acknowledgment and rebuttal shall both be included in the former employee's official employment record.

f. "Permanent information" is formal documentation of a person's current employment status and employment history.

g. "Temporary information" is information which does not make a significant contribution to a person's employment record or which becomes outdated or inaccurate because of the passage of time.

Section 5. Responsibilities.

a. The Director of Human Resources is required to maintain a record of all employees and to develop standards for the establishment and maintenance of employment records.

b. Heads of departments are to ensure that necessary procedures and safeguards are implemented in accordance with this policy.

c. Human Resources Department officers are to be the custodians of personnel records. Custodians are to disclose and withhold employee information in accordance with this policy and are to ensure that information under their control is not accessible to unauthorized persons.

d. The Human Resources Department is to store and control official employment records of inactive employees until the year of the individual's 75th year of birth. At that time, the folders are to be burned or shredded. In addition, the Human Resources Department is to provide information to departments, former employees, and other authorized persons, as prescribed in this policy.

e. The Human Resources Department shall audit this policy's implementation and review complaints and appeals concerning information delays or denials. The Human Resources Department shall also review all subpoenas and other written judicial orders seeking information.

f. All personnel having access to official employment records or to data maintained on the computer files or to the computer-produced reports, directly or through someone else, are to disclose and withhold information in accordance with this policy and are to ensure that information under their control is not accessible to unauthorized persons.

Section 6. Type of Information Kept.

a. This is not an all-inclusive list of information appropriate for maintenance in official employment records. Questions regarding the appropriateness of maintaining other data should be referred to the Human Resources Department. The following types of information are permanent and must be included in official employment records:

(i) Latest employment application;

(ii) Employee notifications regarding appointment, promotion, demotion, involuntary retirement, resignation by reason of abandonment of position, layoff, reassignment, transfer, salary changes (except general pay increases), termination, suspension, disciplinary notices, and temporary assignment in a higher job classification;

(iii) Absence and leave records;

(iv) Last five annual performance evaluations;

(v) Employee-initiated acknowledgments of temporary employment or unusual employment conditions, such as the certificate required of minors;

(vi) Employee requests and responses concerning voluntary retirement, voluntary separation, transfer, demotion, and leaves of absence other than vacation, sick, or personal;

(vii) Employee benefit records;

(viii) Current payroll deduction authorizations including, but not limited to, group life insurance, retirement, medical/hospital insurance, workers' compensation, federal and state withholding tax, earned income tax, union dues, credit union, and tax-sheltered annuities;

(ix) Letters of commendation, cost reduction awards, management improvement awards, exceptional increments, awards for excellence, professional organization or society awards, and any other form of official recognition given an employee that relates to his or her duties and responsibilities; and

(x) Significant training records.

b. The following types of information are temporary and are to be purged from official employment records:

(i) Reference letters;

(ii) Caution, reprimand, admonishment, or warning letters;

(iii) Oral reprimand confirmations;

(iv) Nonpermanent performance evaluations;

(v) Professional affiliations;

(vi) Out-service and in-service training of limited significance to an employee's development; and

(vii) Periodic health examination records required by federal or state regulations.

c. Reference information is subject to access by employees. Only the following employee information may be maintained for reference purposes by departments not maintaining official employment records:

(i) Name and home address;

(ii) Social security number;

(iii) Job classification title;

(iv) Job description, performance objectives, and performance standards;

(v) Data necessary to verify payrolls;

(vi) Attendance records;

(vii) Emergency telephone numbers; and

(viii) Copies of last five performance evaluations.

d. Supervisors' or managers' notes and records on matters involving discipline or performance on specific work assignments may be maintained separately from the official employment record and are not subject to employee access.

e. If a personnel action is amended, only information concerning the amended action is to be maintained. The original personnel action and any rescinded personnel actions are to be removed from an official employment record.

Section 7. Request for Information.

a. Requests for employment information disclosure are to be handled as follows:

(i) An employee's home address may be furnished to police or court officials upon written request showing that an indictment has been returned against an employee or a complaint, information, accusation, or other writ has been filed against an employee and the home address is needed to serve a summons, warrant, or subpoena.

(ii) An employee's social security number and home address may be furnished to taxing authorities upon written request.

(iii) Medical information may be furnished:

(A) When it is needed to aid medical treatment and an employee is not able to provide the information;

(B) To a federal or state investigative agency when requested information is required to verify adherence to regulations.

(iv) Any information available to an employee from his or her own official employment record may be released upon written employee authorization.

(v) The Director of Human Resources is to be notified immediately of the receipt of any subpoena or other written judicial order seeking information not listed in Section 7.a.(i) above. The Human Resources Department, in conjunction with the Company's general

151

counsel, will make a determination as to the response to a subpoena or judicial order. Should a subpoena appear on its face to be relevant to the legal proceeding and not to be overly broad in scope, and without a compelling policy or legal reason to the contrary, the Company will make the requested records available. However, before complying with a subpoena, the employee will be given an opportunity to consult with a private attorney to seek to have the subpoena quashed. Should the Human Resources Department be unable to contact the employee, it will, by certified mail, return receipt requested, mail notification of the subpoena to the employee's last known address.

(vi)   Federal and state law enforcement and investigative agencies are to be provided, upon request, information deemed a public record. Requests from these agencies for nonpublic information are to be honored only if requested information is determined to be relevant to the investigation or audit and is within statutory authority of the requesting agency. Employment records are not to be released. Questions concerning the release of this information should be referred to the Director of Human Resources.

(vii) Following the release of nonpublic information to a federal or state investigative agency, due to a subpoena or otherwise, the Human Resources Department shall notify the employee in writing of what information was released.

(viii) Replies to inquiries from a prospective employer concerning specific reasons for an employee's employment separation are to indicate only whether the separation was voluntary or involuntary. Particular circumstances or issues involved in an involuntary separation are not to be disclosed without the employee's written authorization, or when authorized by the Human Resources Department.

b. Official employment records are to be reviewed at least once every two years or when an employee transfers or is terminated. Information within the files is to be maintained in chronological order. Temporary information four years old or older is to be removed. Oral and written reprimands are to be maintained for two years if no similar incidents occur. Employees are to be notified when documents are removed from their folders and are to be given 10 calendar days to request these documents. Documents not needed for current or pending disciplinary or grievance actions or not requested by employees are to be destroyed.

c. Requests to review official employment records by employees are to be responded to as follows:

(i)   Employees are to be advised that they may choose to travel to the location where the official employment record is maintained. Travel expenses or unpaid leave will not be authorized for this purpose;

(ii)   Upon request, the contents of an employee's official employment record may be duplicated and forwarded for review;

(iii) The Human Resources Department will attach a signed statement to the file certifying that the entire contents of the record were

(iv) copied and contained in the record sent to the employee; and

Employees may be charged reasonable fees for the cost of reproducing material in their official employment records.

Section 8. Access to Inactive Records. The Human Resources Department will provide access to inactive official employment records to clearly identified former employees or persons with letters of authorization from former employees.

Section 9. Administration. The Human Resources Department will review compliance with this policy. Departments will be advised of areas of noncompliance and corrective actions required. If any procedure in this policy conflicts with any provision in a collective bargaining agreement, which provision is otherwise lawful, the provision of the collective bargaining agreement shall control.

MEDICAL RECORDS

MEDICAL RECORD PRIVACY PRINCIPLES

Medical records may contain employee personal details regarding age, life history, family background, medical history, present and past health or illness, mental and emotional health or illness, treatment, accident reports, laboratory reports, and other scientific data from various sources. They may also contain medical providers' notes, prognoses, and reports of the patients' response to treatment. Should this medical information be disclosed, it could cause embarrassment, humiliation, damage to family relationships, or even employment termination, while infringing privacy rights related to speech, associations, and lifestyles.

Medical record technology changes, through third-party payment, government medical care participation, and record-keeping system computerization, have expanded medical information's amount, type, and accessibility. These records may be sought for various reasons. They may be important to legal actions, public health evaluation and occupational health research, third-party payment, employment, credit rating, and other health care provider use.

Employee medical information disclosure to employers may also create privacy problems. This may arise when an employee is disciplined for apparent alcohol or drug abuse before any test is requested. The employer should inform the employee that he or she may vindicate his or her condition by taking an examination. If the employee consents to a medical examination but refuses to provide a written authorization for disclosure of the results, the employer may circumvent the authorization requirement by asking the doctor for an opinion limited to whether the employee is qualified to work.

To minimize potential challenges to discipline imposed following an employee's refusal to release medical information, clear instructions should be given to the employee. The employee should be specifically advised that he or she may be disciplined based on the employer's information then available, even if the employee refuses to submit to an examination or the employee continues to refuse to authorize test result disclosure.

A privacy interest in medical records has been partially acknowledged, and the employee privacy interest in preserving medical record confidentiality has been recognized by federal and state privacy statutes. Society's legitimate need for this information may supersede an employee privacy interest even though an employee's medical records, which may contain intimate personal facts, are entitled to privacy protection. Employee privacy rights must be evaluated against the public interest represented by certain government investigations.

Employers should take precautions to protect medical information confidentiality by restricting access to managerial employees who have a legitimate job-related business interest in obtaining the information. Except in emergency situations, employers should avoid seeking medical information directly from an employee's physician without prior employee consent. Employee hospital records should be accorded similar deference.

Various states restrict dissemination of medical information in the custody of health care providers, and also strictly limit an employer's use and disclosure of employee medical information. Employers should refrain from collecting, maintaining, using, disclosing, or knowingly permitting employees to use or disclose medical information which the employer possesses, without the employee having first signed an authorization permitting this use or disclosure.

Employers must establish appropriate procedures to ensure medical information confidentiality and protection from unauthorized collection, maintenance, use, and disclosure. Procedures may include instructions regarding confidentiality to employees handling files, and security systems restricting file access.

MEDICAL RECORD PROCEDURES

General Considerations

In developing medical record procedures, the employer should consider the following:[5]

1. Medical information disclosure
2. The relationship between the employee and employer regarding any third party requesting the information
3. The employee's privacy interest in not releasing the information
4. The employer's statutory or other duty to disclose the information

[5] Privacy Protection Study commission, Personal Privacy in an Information Society 263 (1977).

5. Identity of the person making the request
6. The request's purpose
7. Restricting disclosure to only necessary information
8. When an employee who is the subject of medical information maintained by an employer requests correction or amendment, the employer should:

    • Disclose to the employee, or to a person designated by him or her, the identity of the medical information's source;

    • Make the correction or amendment within a reasonable time period if the person who was the information's source concurs that the information is inaccurate or incomplete;

    • Establish a procedure for an employee who is the subject of employer medical information to present supplemental information for inclusion in the employer's medical information, provided that the supplemental information's source is also included.

Medical Record Disclosure

Employer authorization for disclosure of medical records should:

1. Be handwritten by the employee
2. Be separate from any other language present on the same page
3. Be signed and dated by the employee
4. State the names, employer functions, or persons authorized to disclose the information
5. State the names, employer functions, persons, or entities authorized to receive the information
6. State the limitations on the medical information's use by those authorized to receive it
7. Provide a date after which the employer is no longer authorized to disclose the information
8. Provide the employee with a copy of the authorization

Medical Record Confidentiality

In maintaining medical record confidentiality, the employer must consider:

1. Record types involved
2. The information
3. The potential for harm should disclosure occur
4. The disclosure's effect on the physician-patient relationship
5. Safeguards against inadvertent or accidental disclosure
6. Statutory or public interest reasons requiring disclosure

MEDICAL RECORD POLICIES

Medical Record Collection Policy

The following policy should be considered by employers regarding employee medical information collection:

MEDICAL RECORD COLLECTION POLICY

Section 1. Medical Record Collection Authorization. For the Company to obtain medical information from an employee, the employee will be required to sign an authorization. The Company shall provide a copy of the authorization to the employee upon demand. The Company shall disclose any limitations on the use of the information to the person to whom it is communicated. The Company shall not be liable for any unauthorized use of the medical information if it has attempted in good faith to communicate the limitations of use. The Company will honor any cancellation or modification of the authorization by the employee upon receipt of written notice.

Section 2. Lack of Medical Record Authorization. If an employee refuses to execute an authorization, the Company will not discriminate against the employee in terms or conditions of employment on the basis of that refusal. However, the Company may take necessary action against an employee, including discipline up to and including termination, in the absence of medical information due to the employee's refusal to sign an authorization. Should the Company be unable to ascertain an employee's ability to perform a job function due to a physical condition, discipline or termination may be appropriate despite the employee's refusal to release medical information. Regardless of whether an employee consents to submit to a test which would evaluate alcohol or drug abuse, the Company has the right to discipline an employee based on other information available to it.

Section 3. No Authorization Required. The Company is not required to obtain employee authorization for release of medical records in the following circumstances:

a. The information is compelled by judicial or administrative process;
b. The information is relevant in a lawsuit, arbitration, grievance, or other claim or challenge to which the Company and employee are parties and in which the employee has placed in issue his or her medical history, medical or physical condition or treatment;
c. For administering and maintaining employee benefit plans, workers' compensation, and for determining eligibility for paid and unpaid leave from work for medical reasons; and
d. Disclosure to a provider of health care.

Medical Record Release

> The following policy should be considered by employers regarding the release of medical information in its possession:

MEDICAL RECORD RELEASE POLICY

Section 1. Release. The Company shall provide medical information that it has collected or maintained regarding its employees. This information shall be provided upon written request of an employee, a former employee, or the employee's designated representative to furnish any medical report pertaining to the employee. This information extends to any medical report arising out of any physical examination by a physician or other health care professional and any hospital or laboratory tests which examinations or tests are required by the Company as a condition of employment or arising out of any injury or disease related to the employee's employment. However, if a physician concludes that presentation of all or any part of an employee's medical record directly to the employee will result in serious medical harm to the employee, he or she shall so indicate on the medical record, in which case a copy shall be given to a physician designated in writing by the employee.

Section 2. Cost Reimbursement. The Company may require the employee, former employee, or the employee's designated representative to pay the reasonable cost of furnishing medical report copies.

Medical Record Confidentiality

The following policy should be considered by employers regarding employee medical information confidentiality:

MEDICAL RECORD CONFIDENTIALITY POLICY

The Company shall maintain medical information confidentiality regarding applicants, employees, and former employees. It shall furnish only medical information to a physician designated in writing by the applicant, employee, or former employee. However, the Company may use or supply medical examination information in response to subpoenas, requests to the Company by any governmental agency, and in arbitration or litigation of any claim or action involving the Company.

5

WORKPLACE MEDICAL CONCERNS

Employee privacy interests present in workplace medical concerns are gaining importance through the growing awareness of alcohol and drug abuse and through the uncertainty over acquired immune deficiency syndrome (AIDS). Employees and employers are increasingly confronted with serious questions regarding how medical privacy concerns should be balanced. This chapter reviews medical privacy concerns arising out of physical examinations, smoking, employee assistance programs, alcohol and drug abuse, and AIDS.

PHYSICAL EXAMINATIONS

PHYSICAL EXAMINATION PRIVACY PRINCIPLES

The employer's right to require applicants to undergo a physical examination is considered basic to the hiring process. Due to their cost, physical examinations are usually administered at the final hiring process step. Situations also arise that necessitate requiring physical examinations during the employment relationship.

Employers may, unless restricted by a collective bargaining agreement, require employees to have physical examinations under legitimate job-related circumstances. This need may arise where an employee desires to return to work following an accident, sick leave, or extended layoff, has exercised a bid on a job requiring greater physical effort, and so forth. Regarding employee privacy concerns, this right is not absolute exercisable at the whim of the employer. It cannot be arbitrarily insisted upon without reasonable grounds. Unreasonable requests for physical examinations could expose employers to liability under federal and state FEP statutes.

PHYSICAL EXAMINATION PROCEDURES

To ensure that proper medical information is obtained, employers should consider the following concerning physical examinations:

1. Establishing relationships with one or more physicians because the physician:
   - Understands the job's physical requirements
   - Is able to provide a faster conclusion regarding employment eligibility
   - Is familiar with required paperwork
   - Provides a more convenient means for dialogue with the human resources staff
2. Employing a full- or part-time physician on a retainer and/or one of a group of physicians.

PHYSICAL EXAMINATION POLICIES

Physical Examination Required

The following policy should be considered for employers to notify employees of the employers' right to require physical examinations:

PHYSICAL EXAMINATION POLICY

To determine medical fitness for employment, the Company may require employee physical examinations, when it is deemed advisable for health and safety, by a Company-employed physician. The Company may also require applicants to be physically examined at the Company's expense. Should an employee be found medically unfit to work at his or her assigned job, the Company will furnish the employee a copy of the physician's report or a physician's statement. Any applicant or employee may also be examined at his or her own expense by a physician selected by him or her and the physician's report may be submitted to the Company for consideration.

Physical Examinations for Contagious Diseases or for
Sanitary Measures

The following policy should be considered where physical examinations are necessitated by a contagious disease or sanitary measure:

PHYSICAL EXAMINATION REQUIRED FOR CONTAGIOUS DISEASES OR FOR SANITARY MEASURES

Section 1. Contagious Diseases. The Company may require physical examinations for contagious diseases. To protect the lives and well-being of all, employees with untreated or incurable contagious diseases may be given an unpaid medical leave, laid off, or terminated, depending upon the medical evaluation.

Section 2. Sanitary Measures. The Company may require a physical examination of any employee should it appear necessary as a sanitary or safety measure. The physical examination shall be made by the Company's physician at the Company's expense.

Physical Examination after Accident or Sickness

The following policy should be considered where a physical examination is necessitated by an employee's accident or sickness:

PHYSICAL EXAMINATION AFTER ACCIDENT OR SICKNESS

Section 1.   Physical Examination Required.   If an employee has been absent because of accident or sickness, the Company may require a physical examination by a physician of the Company's choice. Following the examination, if it is determined that the sickness or accident may subject the employee to other or continued sickness or accidents, he or she will not be allowed to return to work.

Section 2.   Result Disputes.   Should the employee disagree with the Company physician's decision, he or she may be examined by a physician of his or her own choosing, provided that notification of this intent is given to the Company within three (3) calendar days after the Company has denied the right to return to work. Any costs incurred by this physician will be paid by the employee.

If the employee's physician indicates that the employee can return to work, the Company will be notified in writing by the physician making the determination. The notification must be given to the Company not later than thirty (30) calendar days from the date the employee has been notified that he or she has been denied the right to return to work.

If the matter cannot be resolved, the Company's and the employee's physician will select a third physician to whom to submit their respective findings. The third physician may examine the employee and make a determination concerning the employee's status. Any expense incurred by the third physician will be shared equally by the Company and the employee. The third physician's finding will be considered by the Company in determining whether the employee should be returned to work.

Physical Examinations for Employees in Hazardous Jobs

The following policy should be considered where physical examinations are necessitated by hazardous jobs:

PHYSICAL EXAMINATIONS FOR EMPLOYEES IN HAZARDOUS JOBS

To protect employees while working on jobs that may constitute health hazards, employees may, upon the Company's request or the employee's, be given a Company-paid physical examination. If the examination is made by a Company physician, the physical examination report, upon the employee's written request, will be sent to the employee's physician.

Physical Examination Employee Compensation

The following policy should be considered where the employer determines that it would be appropriate to compensate an employee for undergoing a physical examination at its request:

PHYSICAL EXAMINATION EMPLOYEE COMPENSATION

The Company may require employee physical examinations or tests made by its physician at its expense. Where possible, the physical examination will be scheduled during the employee's normal working hours. The Company will compensate the employee for the time involved at the employee's applicable pay rate for a Company-required physical examination that occurs during the employee's normal working hours or outside the employee's normal working hours.

Physical Examination Information Available to
Employee's Physician

The following policy should be considered in disclosing the employer's physical examination information to the employee's physician:

PHYSICAL EXAMINATION INFORMATION AVAILABLE TO EMPLOYEE'S PHYSICIAN

Employee physical examinations may be arranged by the Company only when necessary and only after notifying the employee with an explanation of the specific reasons for the examination. Report copies of these physical examinations and medical treatments will be maintained by the Company in its Medical Department and will be available to the employee's physician, if authorized in writing by the employee.

Physical Examination Confidentiality

> The following policy should be considered in maintaining physical examination confidentiality:

PHYSICAL EXAMINATION CONFIDENTIALITY

The Company will maintain physical examination result confidentiality. These results shall be furnished only to the employee's designated physician upon the employee's written authorization; provided that the Company may use or supply physical examination results in response to subpoenas, requests to the Company by any governmental agency authorized by law to obtain these reports, and in arbitration or litigation of any claim or action involving the Company.

Physical Examination Results Dispute: Medical Arbitrator

> The following policy should be considered as a means to resolve a dispute regarding the physical examination results that may arise between the employer's physician and the applicant's/ employee's physician:

PHYSICAL EXAMINATION RESULTS DISPUTE: MEDICAL ARBITRATOR

Section 1. Physical Examinations Required. An applicant, before being hired, must meet certain job-related health and physical fitness standards as determined by a physical examination given by a Company-designated physician. After employment, periodic physical examinations may be offered or required to aid an employee in improving health or to enable the Company to ensure its employees' health.

Section 2. Results. An applicant/employee, upon request, shall have the opportunity to discuss his or her physical examination's results with the Company's physician. Upon the applicant's/employee's request, the information will be made available to his or her personal physician.

Section 3. Result Disputes. Should the Company's physician determine that an applicant/employee cannot perform the job applied for or currently held because of an existing medical condition, and should a dispute arise between the Company's physician and the employee's personal physician regarding this determination, a complaint may be filed with the Human Resources Department.

If the complaint is not resolved by the Human Resources Department, the applicant/employee, the Company's physician, and the applicant's/employee's personal physician shall exchange x-rays, laboratory test reports, and physical examination reports within ten (10) calendar days of the date the complaint was filed with the Human Resources Department.

If, after exchanging of x-rays and reports, final agreement cannot be reached regarding the medical findings and conclusions, the applicant/employee may, within fourteen (14) calendar days after the exchange, refer the dispute to the Company's President, who shall attempt to resolve the problem by examining all available medical evidence.

If a dispute still exists regarding the applicant's/employee's medical condition after the Company President's review, the dispute may be presented to an impartial medical arbitrator selected by mutual agreement of the parties in accordance with the following:

a. Within fourteen (14) calendar days following the dispute's referral to the Company's President, all x-rays and reports shall be forwarded to the medical arbitrator.

b. Within fourteen (14) calendar days thereafter, the medical arbitrator shall conduct whatever employee examination is deemed necessary and appropriate, and shall meet with the two physicians, along with any medical experts, to discuss the findings.

c. Within fourteen (14) calendar days thereafter, the medical arbitrator shall submit to the Company and the applicant/employee a written determination.

d. Any of the time limits provided herein may be extended by the parties' mutual written agreement.

e. The charges and expenses of the medical arbitrator shall be paid equally by the parties.
f. The determination of the medical arbitrator shall be final and binding on the parties and the applicant/employee involved.

SMOKING

SMOKING PRIVACY PRINCIPLES

Workplace smoking is changing rapidly. Employers are increasingly taking steps to curtail workplace smoking. Permitting or not regulating workplace smoking makes employers vulnerable to challenges by nonsmoking employees. Mounting concern over smoking's effects on the health, productivity, and morale of smokers and nonsmokers has combined with changing social attitudes about smoking to reverse the notion that smoking is an acceptable public practice. In addition, certain workplace environments, such as around computers, must be kept free of smoke or other pollution. Awards for unemployment, disability, and medical treatment have been made to nonsmokers, and union grievances under collective bargaining agreements are increasingly dealing with this issue.

As a privacy issue, smoking is becoming an activity that an employee does within the confines of his or her home, but not at the workplace or in public. Privacy questions concern the employer's liability if smoking is or is not restricted, and whether only nonsmokers can be hired.

While discrimination against smokers is not prohibited by federal and state FEP statutes, it certainly affects a privacy-related interest. It may be a non-job-related criterion that controls employment distribution, especially when employers do not hire smokers or restrict smoking outside the workplace. By not confining job-relatedness criteria to the workplace, employers could deny opportunities based on what occurs outside the workplace. When using employment as an incentive to control how employees act at home, employers decide or circumscribe what is done in private. This could be a guise under which to discriminate if statistics establish that certain minority, national origin, or age groups smoke more than others.

SMOKING PROCEDURES

In developing workplace smoking procedures, the following should be considered:

1. Establish a smoking policy, which may be either voluntary or a total prohibition

2. For unionized employers, meet with the union to discuss the smoking policy

3. Consult employees for their input

4. Communicate the policy

5. Require all employees to follow the policy

6. Establish smoking and nonsmoking areas

7. Make smoke cessation classes available for persons who want to stop smoking

8. Improve ventilation to minimize smoking's health hazard

9. Where employees have a medically proven reaction to smoke, separate those persons from smokers, but do not terminate them

10. Where smoking presents a work safety hazard, due to paints, chemicals, or explosives, adopt and implement a smoking ban that is reasonable

11. Investigate smoking complaints

SMOKING POLICIES

The following should be considered in dealing with workplace smoking:

SMOKING POLICY

Section 1. Purpose and Background. This policy is designed to promote employee health and safety and the conduct of Company business. It is not intended to totally prohibit smoking on the Company's premises, but does restrict it to certain areas.

Smoking poses a significant risk to the smoker's and nonsmoker's health. It can damage sensitive technical equipment and can be a safety hazard. In sufficient concentrations, sidestream smoke can be annoying to nonsmokers. It may be harmful to individuals with heart and respiratory diseases or allergies related to tobacco smoke.

Smoking is a complex problem that concerns elements of a psychological and physiological addiction. Many individuals require assistance to eliminate smoking from their lives. It is not a problem that can be solved completely by prohibition or restriction. This policy is intended to assist employees in finding a reasonable accommodation between those who do not smoke and those who do, and demonstrates the Company's desire to improve the health of all employees.

Section 2. Policy. It is the Company's policy to respect the nonsmoker's and the smoker's rights in Company buildings and facilities. When these rights conflict, the Company and its employees should endeavor to find a reasonable accommodation. When an accommodation is not possible, the nonsmoker's rights should prevail.

Section 3. Prohibited Areas. Smoking is not permitted:

a. In areas with sensitive equipment, computer systems, or where records and supplies would be exposed to hazard from fires, ashes, or smoke;

b. Where combustible fumes can collect, as in garage and storage areas, areas where chemicals are used, and all other designated areas where an occupational safety or health hazard might exist;

c. In confined areas of general access, as in libraries, medical facilities, cashier waiting lines, elevators, restrooms, stairwells, copy rooms, lobbies, waiting rooms, fitness centers, and so forth;

d. Where Company premises are frequently visited by customers, such as public offices and customer service areas; and

e. The Company may designate other locations where smoking specifically is not permitted.

Section 4. Work Areas. In work areas where space is shared by two or more persons, an effort shall be made to accommodate individual smoking preferences to the degree reasonably possible. When requested, managers and supervisors shall make a reasonable attempt to separate persons who smoke from those who do not.

Employees may designate their private offices as smoking or nonsmoking areas. Visitors to private work areas should honor the employee's wishes.

In Company vehicles, including Company-sponsored van pools, smoking shall be permitted only when there is no objection from one or more of the occupants.

Section 5. Areas of Common Use. In meetings and enclosed locations, including conference rooms and classrooms, smoking will not be permitted. Breaks and appropriate access to public areas may be scheduled to accommodate smoker needs.

In enclosed common-use locations, including cafeterias, dining areas, employee lounges, and auditoriums, smoking shall be permitted only in identified smoking sections, providing there is adequate ventilation and they are not normal customer areas. Smoking is permitted in corridors. Employees and visitors are expected to honor the smoking and nonsmoking designations and to be considerate of nonsmokers in their vicinity.

The following policy should be considered in banning workplace smoking altogether by implementing the ban in phases:

SMOKING BAN POLICY

Section 1. Purpose and Background. This Smoking Ban Policy is designed to provide the Company's employees with a more healthy workplace environment. Implementation of this policy is a direct result of several compelling health and safety issues:

a. An increasing number of health conscious people are legitimately concerned about the impact on their health by smoke in the workplace.
b. Smoking poses a significant risk to the smoker's and nonsmoker's health.
c. The U.S. Surgeon General has defined nicotine as an addicting substance, and has released compelling statistics on the impact of smoke inhalation (active and passive) on our health.
d. Smokers and nonsmokers will benefit from a firm, definitive, yet thoughtfully implemented policy.
e. Smoke can damage sensitive equipment and be a safety hazard.

Section 2. Objective. An essential part of this policy's implementation is the recognition that the elimination of smoking in all Company facilities and Company owned vehicles is done for the benefit of all employees, guests, and friends of the Company. The hazards of smoking have an impact on all employees and require the cooperation of all employees.

Section 3. Implementation. Maintaining the Company's commitment to its employees as its single greatest asset, the Company is implementing its policy as follows:

a. *Phase 1* is a period of employee education. Education consisting of communication of this policy, assistance for smokers in dealing with the smoking restrictions, and education of nonsmokers about their role in this effort.

b. *Phase 2* is a six-month transition period, beginning (date) , during which indoor smoking at all locations will be permitted only in *specifically designated areas*. These areas are listed below:

(List permitted smoking areas)

_____

_____

_____

_____

c. *Phase 3*, beginning (date) , a *complete ban* on smoking in all Company facilities will be imposed. Additionally, during Phase 3, all smoking in Company-owned vehicles will be prohibited.

EMPLOYEE ASSISTANCE PROGRAMS (EAP)

EAP PRIVACY PRINCIPLES

Employee assistance programs (EAPs) help employees and their families to recognize and overcome personal problems that interfere with employee work performance. They are an extension of the performance evaluation process. Problem areas covered may involve job dissatisfaction, supervisor or coworker conflicts, job performance anxiety, alcohol and drug abuse, emotional problems, marital problems, gambling problems, financial problems, and so forth. Because employer confidentiality is required to make EAPs function properly, confidentiality breaches may result in employee privacy litigation.

EAPs require considerable planning and operational expertise to function properly. In addition to administering the EAP, various actions must be taken to ensure that the program operates efficiently. Efficient operation means that the program prevents employee problems and identifies, treats, and rehabilitates those employees who are troubled.

EAP PROCEDURES

EAPs can be developed by the employer or contracted through agencies providing such programs. Privacy and confidentiality are essential EAP elements. Collection, maintenance, use, or disclosure of EAP information may impact privacy interests present in speech, beliefs, association, and lifestyle. Unless privacy and confidentiality can be guaranteed, the EAP will not be utilized by employees. In developing an EAP, the following should be considered:

1. Confidentiality and privacy in:
   - Recordkeeping
   - Coding records to prevent inadvertent identification of those who are enrolled
   - Limiting supervisor access
   - Keeping EAP records separate from employee personnel or medical records
2. Communicating EAP services to employees and their families by:

- Employee education
- Orientating managers, supervisors, and union representatives

3. Procedures for individuals referred by managers, supervisors, and/or union representatives
4. Procedures for use by employees and their families
5. The EAP's location
6. The EAP's coordination with medical and disability benefit plans
7. Outside agency versus Company provision of the EAP regarding:
   - The EAP provider's malpractice liability insurance
   - The EAP staff's qualifications

EAP POLICY

EMPLOYEE ASSISTANCE PROGRAM POLICY

The following policy should be considered in offering an EAP:

EMPLOYEE ASSISTANCE PROGRAM POLICY

Section 1. Purpose. The Company has always been concerned with its employees' health and well-being. Because of these concerns, an Employee Assistance Program (EAP) has been developed to aid employees who develop medical or behavioral problems. Some of these problems include alcohol and drug abuse, marital, family, gambling, legal, financial, psychological, medical, or behavioral difficulties.

Section 2. General Coverage. Employee effectiveness can deteriorate for many reasons. Often it is personal or family problems that affects job performance. The Company's EAP is designed to help employees with these problems, including directing them to appropriate professional services. Employees or their family members who are suffering from any type of personal problem are encouraged to voluntarily seek diagnostic counseling and treatment services available under the EAP.

Section 3. Alcohol and Drug Abuse Coverage. The following are aspects of the Company's EAP regarding alcohol and drug abuse:

a. Alcoholism along with drug abuse is a significant problem;

b. The Company recognizes alcohol and drug abuse as treatable diseases;

c. An employee with an alcohol or drug abuse problem will receive the same careful consideration that is extended to employees suffering from any other disease; and

d. For the purposes of the EAP, *alcohol and drug abuse* is defined as the continuing use of alcoholic beverages or drugs that definitely and repeatedly interferes with health or job performance.

Section 4. Job Performance Coverage. The following are aspects of the Company's EAP regarding job performance:

a. Job performance is the key to recognition of a need for EAP services; and

b. Employees whose deteriorating job performance does not respond to normal corrective action should be referred to the EAP, if the supervisor believes that the poor job performance is caused by a medical or behavioral problem.

Section 5. Supervisor Participation. Supervisors should understand that they are not expected to be qualified to diagnose alcoholism, drug abuse, other personal problems, or to make judgments about the behavioral problem causes. It is the employee who is responsible for accepting and complying with a supervisor's referral to the EAP. This employee responsibility includes:

a. Following the treatment prescribed; and

b. An employee's refusal to accept diagnosis and treatment will be handled in the same way that similar refusals or treatment failures are handled for other illnesses, when the result of the refusals or failures continues to affect job performance.

Section 6. Confidentiality. All records and activities within the EAP will be preserved in accordance with Company policies on privacy and confidentiality of sensitive records.

ALCOHOL AND DRUG ABUSE

ALCOHOL AND DRUG PRIVACY PRINCIPLES

Employers are developing alcohol and drug abuse programs to increase workplace productivity and safety. Medical testing procedures are a significant part of these programs.

Regardless of the benefits that testing may provide concerning workplace productivity and safety, it presents important employee privacy considerations. By its very nature, testing intrudes upon the employee's solitude and physical integrity. When testing is administered to detect employee alcohol or drug use, intrusiveness increases in complexity and degree. Like all other individual rights, however, employee privacy is not absolute. It must be balanced against competing employer interests and objectives.

Employee privacy concerns consistently arise in any private or public sector employer's involvement with alcohol and drug programs. Private and public sector employers implementing these programs are subject to privacy limitations under the United States Constitution and certain state constitutions. Statutory obligations may exist regarding an employer's requirement to rehabilitate employees who abuse alcohol or drugs.

Various federal and state FEP statutes may affect drug testing when it has a disproportionate adverse effect on minorities, certain national origin groups, and so forth. Searching or testing employees may subject employers to liability under various litigation theories, including invasion of privacy, defamation, and false imprisonment. Invasion of privacy may provide protection in safeguarding an employee's solitude, seclusion, and private affairs. Before conducting a drug search, an employer should limit the employee's privacy expectation by giving prior notice that searches can occur. When the employer creates a privacy expectation through a handbook or employment policy, it may be required to follow that policy. The search's scope may also impose employer liability. Finally, publicly disclosing private facts about a drug test's results may impose liability.

ALCOHOL AND DRUG PROCEDURES

Initial Considerations

Employers contemplating the adoption of alcohol and drug testing programs should seriously consider the programs' scope,
purpose, and effect regarding:[1]

1. Drug testing necessity

2. Employee group or category to be tested

3. Giving notice to all affected employees

4. Receiving employee consent to test and to disclose test
    results

5. Selecting a reputable laboratory to analyze employee
    samples

6. The employer's response to employees who have a positive
    test result or who refuse to take a test

7. Arranging for a confirming test on positive samples

8. Guarding against information disclosure about employees
    obtained through the tests

9. Limiting alcohol or drug testing to situations where on-
    the-job impairment is evident

10. Having supervisors document behavior that suggests alco-
     hol or drug impairment

11. Interviewing employees about illnesses or prescription
     drugs that may adversely affect their job performance

12. Implementing or strengthening restrictions on the use or
     possession of alcohol or drugs on employer property dur-
     ing work hours

13. Ensuring that the facts and circumstances that created the
     reasonable suspicion are documented where testing is per-
     formed based on a reasonable suspicion

14. Providing an opportunity for the union to participate in
     establishing an alcohol and drug testing program, by
     bargaining with the union over the changes in work rules

---

[1] See Littler, Mendelson, Fastiff & Tichy, *Responding to Drug and Alcohol Abuse in the
Workplace,* in The 1987 Employer B, B-31 (1987). Littler, Mendelson, Fastiff & Tichy
prepare this publication on an annual basis for Business Laws, Inc. of 8228 Mayfield
Road in Chesterland, Ohio 44026; telephone (216) 729-7996. This publication is an
excellent reference source for human resource professionals and attorneys as an annual update of employment laws.

or practices resulting from adopting a testing program under a collective bargaining agreement.

Minimizing Liability

To minimize employer liability for employee privacy claims
arising out of alcohol and drug testing, the following should be
considered:[2]

1. *Obtain a release/authorization.* Before an applicant/
    employee is tested for alcohol or drugs, the employer
    should obtain test consent. The consent form should solicit
    information regarding prescription drug use or nonpre-
    scription medication to eliminate false positives. For exam-
    ple, therapeutic cold medicines, such as Contac and
    Sudafed, can create a false positive for amphetamine use.
    The consent form may help protect the employer against
    claims for invasion of privacy, defamation, false imprison-
    ment, assault and battery, and so forth

2. *Do a follow-up test.* An initial screening test indicating a
    positive result should be verified by a confirmation test for
    all employees. Employers may wish to perform confirma-
    tion tests for applicants where:
    • There are few applicants, to minimize an additional
      test's costs
    • The initial test is positive regarding an otherwise highly
      qualified applicant
    • The applicant desires confirmation in contesting an ad-
      verse employment decision

3. *Safeguard the specimen.* The specimen should be marked
    in the applicant's/employee's presence and a documented
    chain of custody maintained to ensure that the specimen is
    correct. Selecting a reliable laboratory is essential.

4. *Restrict test disclosure.* Test results should not be publi-
    cized. Even when the drug tests are considered accurate
    and there is no risk of publication of a false fact, they
    should not be disclosed.

5. *Use split samples.* The specimen should initially be split
    into two samples. Every sample should be preserved for a
    reasonable time period; such as 60 to 90 days. During this

---

[2] *See* Redeker & Segal, *Drug and Alcohol Testing: Legal and Practical Considerations,* 7
Bureau of Nat'l Affairs Communicator 2, 20 (Fall 1987).

period, the employee who provided the sample should be permitted to have the sample evaluated independently by a confirmation test at his or her own expense. An employee who has the opportunity to confirm the test results independently may be less likely to challenge those results. Where applicants are not permitted independently to confirm their test results because they may not be informed of the test's results, a separate sample should be retained in case the applicant challenges an adverse employment decision.

ALCOHOL AND DRUG POLICIES

Letter Introducing Company Alcohol and Drug Policy

In introducing the employer's alcohol and drug policy, the following letter to employees should be considered:

Dear __(Employee's Name)__ :

We are all aware that alcohol and drug abuse is a major problem throughout our society. As you know, the Company has made a commitment for a work environment free from alcohol and drug substances. The Company's primary objectives are employee health and safety, along with fulfilling obligations to the public and customers, protecting private and public property, and preserving the confidence placed in the Company.

The Company has been carefully considering how best to fulfill these responsibilities. As a result, the Company has prepared an Alcohol and Drug Abuse Policy. The Company's purpose is to discourage alcohol and drug abuse so all can benefit from a healthy and safe workplace. Here are some highlights of the Alcohol and Drug Abuse Policy that will become effective on __(Date)__ :

1. *Voluntary Assistance.* An employee who voluntarily seeks assistance on a timely basis through the Employee Assistance Program (EAP) or the Company's Medical Department for any problem, including an alcohol- or drug-related problem, may do so without jeopardizing employment status, providing that prescribed treatment is followed and work performance is acceptable. In some cases temporary reassignment may be necessary.

2. *Alcoholic Beverages.* Employees shall not consume alcoholic beverages during regular or overtime working hours, during paid or unpaid meal periods when the employee will be returning to work following the meal period, or during working hours when representing the Company away from Company facilities. Also, employees shall not report to work under the influence of alcoholic beverages or possess alcoholic beverages on Company property.

3. *Other Substances Which Alter Mental or Physical Capacity.* Use, possession, sale, or purchase of other substances that may alter mental or physical capacity while on the job or on Company property is prohibited. Employees shall not report to work under the influence of these substances.

4. *Searches.* To help ensure a work environment free of alcohol and drugs, the Company may search an employee's personal effects located on Company property and the employee's work area.

5. *Physical/Clinical Tests.* Employees may be physically examined and/or clinically tested:
   a. When there are reasonable grounds for believing an employee is either under the influence of or is improperly using alcohol or drugs in violation of the policy;
   b. As part of Company-required physical examinations; or
   c. As a follow-up to a rehabilitation program.

6. *Prescribed Treatment.* An employee undergoing prescribed medical treatment with a substance that may alter physical or mental capacity must report this to the Medical Department.

7. *Reporting Violations.* An employee who observes or has knowledge of a violation of the Alcohol and Drug Abuse Policy by another employee or others has an obligation promptly to report the violation to his or her immediate supervisor and/or the Human Resources Department. Any supervisor who receives this report or who observes this violation must report the information to the responsible supervisor and/or the Human Resources Department.

8. *Imminent Threat to Safety.* In any instance where there exists an imminent threat to safety of persons or property as a result of apparent unfitness for duty, an employee shall immediately contact his or her supervisor and the Human Resources Department.

9. *Disciplinary Action.* Unlawful involvement with alcohol and drugs on or off the job is a serious conduct breach. Violations of the Alcohol and Drug Abuse Policy will result in disciplinary action up to and including termination.

10. *Law Enforcement Notification.* Where criminal violations are involved or suspected, appropriate law enforcement agencies will be notified.

11. *Applicability.* The Alcohol and Drug Abuse Policy applies to all Company employees, regardless of work location or employment status.

All of us have a responsibility for diligent, professional performance, and conduct that demonstrates trust of the public and our fellow employees. Because of this, please cooperate with the Company in implementing this policy so we can provide a healthy and safe workplace.

This is an important topic, and I am sure each of us can understand the need to adhere strictly to the requirements outlined herein. If you have any questions concerning this matter, please contact your supervisor promptly.

Thank you for your continued cooperation.

Very truly yours,

_____
President

Alcohol and Drug Policy: Basic Statement

> The following should be considered by employers as an introductory alcohol and drug abuse policy that should be added to as conditions warrant:

ALCOHOL AND DRUGS

Alcoholic beverages are not permitted on the Company's premises, at Company-sponsored functions, or in Company-owned vehicles. Illegal controlled substances are not permitted on the Company's premises, at Company-sponsored functions, or in Company-owned vehicles. This policy applies to any prescription drugs that may have an adverse impact on an employee's ability to work safely while using these drugs. It is the employee's responsibility to have his or her physician's permission to work while using the prescription medicine and to inform the Company of this so it can make an evaluation.

Alcohol and Drug Policy: Comprehensive Policy

> The following alcohol and drug policy should be considered by a large employer:[3]

---

[3] *See generally* Edison Electric Institute Human Resource Management Division, EEI Guide to Effective Drug and Alcohol Fitness for Duty Policy Development (rev'd Aug. 1985), as adapted by GPU Nuclear Corporation courtesy of James Troebliger, Manager of Human Resources.

ALCOHOL AND DRUGS

Section 1. Purpose. To support the Company's commitment to protect the health and safety of the public and its employees, this policy is designed for maintaining an alcohol- and drug-free workplace.

Section 2. Applicability. This policy has Company-wide applicability.

Section 3. Definitions.

  a. *Alcohol.* Any beverage that may be legally sold and consumed and that has an alcoholic content in excess of .5% by volume.

  b. *Disciplinary action.* Action taken against an employee found to be in violation of Company policies.

  c. *Drug.* Any physical- or mind-altering substance or any "controlled substance" or "controlled dangerous substance" as defined by federal and state statutes. These include, but are not limited to, any non-prescribed drug, narcotic, heroin, cocaine, or marijuana, or a prescribed drug which is abused or not used in accordance with a physician's evaluation.

  d. *Employee.* All employees regardless of work location or employment status.

  e. *Responsible supervisor.* The supervisor to whom the employee reports.

Section 4. Requirements. Employees shall not consume alcoholic beverages during regular or overtime working hours, during paid or unpaid meal periods when the employee will be returning to work following the meal period, or during working hours when representing the Company away from Company facilities. Additionally, employees shall not report to work under the influence of alcoholic beverages or possess alcoholic beverages on Company property.

The use, possession, sale, or purchase of other substances which may alter mental or physical capacity, which substances include, but are not limited to, nonprescribed drugs, narcotics, marijuana, or other "controlled substances" or "controlled dangerous substances" as defined by federal or state statutes while on the job or on Company property is prohibited. Employees shall not report to work under the influence of these substances.

The unlawful involvement with alcohol or drugs on or off the job is a serious conduct breach. Each employee has an obligation to advise the Company of any known violations of these requirements. Violations of these requirements will result in disciplinary action up to and including termination.

The Company also applies the intent of these requirements to maintain a safe work environment free of alcohol and drugs to all contractors, business invitees, visitors, and guests to Company property.

Section 5. Drug and Alcohol Testing. To help ensure an alcohol- and drug-free workplace, the Company may search an employee's personal effects located on Company property, the work area of an employee, and physically examine and/or clinically test employees for the presence of alcohol or drugs during working hours.

Employees may be physically examined and/or clinically tested for the presence of alcohol or drugs:

a. Where there are reasonable grounds for believing an employee is either under the influence of or is suspected of using alcohol or drugs;
b. As part of any Company-required physical examination;
c. As a follow-up to a rehabilitative program;
d. On a random basis where health and safety requirements necessitate this.

If the alcohol or drug test reveals positive results, the employee will be suspended pending joint evaluation by the affected manager, Human Resources Department, and Medical Department. Employees whose physical examinations and/or test results are positive are subject to disciplinary action up to and including termination. If the test results are negative, the matter will be closed.

All applicants and all Company employees whose assignment will make them an "employee" shall be physically examined and/or chemically tested for the presence of alcohol and drugs. The employment process will be terminated for all individuals whose examinations and/or tests are positive.

Section 6. Voluntary Assistance. An employee who voluntarily seeks assistance on a timely basis through the Employee Assistance Program or the Company's Health Services Department for an alcohol- or drug-related problem, prior to the Company identifying the problem, may do so without jeopardizing their employment status, providing that prescribed treatment is followed and work performance is acceptable. In some cases temporary reassignment may be necessary.

Section 7. Prescribed Treatment. If an employee is undergoing a prescribed medical treatment with a substance that may alter physical or mental capacity, he or she must report this to the Medical Department.

Section 8. Reporting Violations. Any supervisor who observes or receives a violation report must, as soon as practicable, report the information to the responsible supervisor, and/or the Human Resources Department.

Any employee who observes or has knowledge of a violation, whether by an employee or others, has an obligation promptly to report this to his or her immediate supervisor and/or the Human Resources Department.

Section 9. Imminent Threat to Safety. In any instance where there exists an imminent threat to safety of persons or property, an employee shall immediately contact the manager, supervisor, or the Human Resources Department.

Section 10. Responsible Supervisor Action. Supervisors must assure that all employees are familiar with and comply with this policy. They must notify the Human Resources Department of any known or suspected violation. When a responsible supervisor observes or receives a report of a possible violation, he or she shall:

a. Confirm that the Human Resources Department has been advised.
b. Follow further directions of the Human Resources Department, which may include conducting an initial evaluation.

187

c. If the responsible supervisor is asked to conduct an initial evaluation, he or she shall report the results to the Human Resources Department. If no apparent violation has occurred, the matter will be closed.

d. Determine in conjunction with the Human Resources Department whether it is advisable or necessary to suspend an employee, with or without pay, or reassign him or her pending completion of the investigation.

e. Recommend any proposed disciplinary action and ensure that the recommendation is reviewed, approved, and implemented by the Human Resources Department.

When a supervisor observes or receives a report of a possible violation by others, including contractors, business invitees, visitors or guests, he or she shall:

a. Advise the individual's responsible supervisor if that individual is a contractor or sponsor for access to the facility of a business invitee, visitor, or guest.

b. Advise the Human Resources Department.

c. Provide further assistance or cooperation as may be requested.

Section 11. Human Resources.   It is the Human Resource Department's responsibility to:

a. Review recommended disciplinary actions and ensure that the actions are in accordance and consistent with Company procedure.

b. Assemble a complete, comprehensive, and coherent file on the incident, where personnel action is taken.

c. Ensure that appropriate procedures and policies are communicated to all employees.

d. Ensure that appropriate division/departments are notified and participate in the recommendations resulting from investigations.

Section 12. Other Responsibilities.   The following are other responsibilities in administering this policy and are not intended to supersede other requirements:

a. All employees must:
   (i)   Become informed and comply with the policy;
   (ii) Cooperate with investigations;
   (iii) Report any known policy violation; and
   (iv) Immediately respond to imminent threat to the safety of person or property.

b. Department managers must:
   (i)   Ensure that all subordinates are conversant with and comply with the policy; and
   (ii) Review investigative reports and disciplinary action recommendations.

c. Human Resources must:

(i) Communicate this procedure and policy to all employees, including new hires;

(ii) Arrange for alcohol and drug testing; and

(iii) Review investigative reports and recommend disciplinary action.

d. Medical Department must:

(i) Supervise physical examinations and testing for presence of alcohol or drugs; and

(ii) Apprise the Human Resources Department and the responsible supervisor of the results of any the examinations or tests.

URINE DRUG SCREEN COLLECTION PROCEDURE

The following procedure should be used in collecting applicant/employee urine samples for alcohol or drug analysis:

URINE DRUG SCREEN COLLECTION PROCEDURE

1. Before collecting:
    a. *Identification*. Positively identify the patient by checking a photograph identification.
        (i) This can be a driver's license, a photograph identification, a United States passport, or other official document that has a photograph.
        (ii) When the photograph identification has been presented and checked for authenticity, initial the appropriate space on the request form.
        (iii) If the patient cannot be positively identified, DO NOT COLLECT THE SAMPLE. Contact the Human Resources Department.
    b. *Medical-Legal Specimen Control Record*. Record correctly the patient's name, age, sex, and requesting physician, along with a chain of custody form.
    c. *Company release form*. Have the employee read and sign this form, listing all over-the-counter and prescription medications by brand names. If the brand name is unknown, describe the medication and note: "Brand name unknown."
    d. *Specimen labeling*. Label the specimen container cap with a Selex marker before handing it to the patient.
2. Collection:
    a. Ask the applicant/employee to leave behind pocket books, bags, coats, extra sweaters, and so forth.
    b. Accompany the applicant/employee to the restroom and do not leave the area during collection. Unless specifically instructed, do not go into the washroom with the applicant/employee.
3. After collection:
    a. Take the specimen from the patient, be sure the cap is secure, then seal with the evidence security tape.
        (i) When sealing, place the tape across the lid and down one side;
        (ii) Then put date, time and your initials on the tape with a Selex pen.
    b. Record date collected on the request form.
    c. Record date of collection, time, test requested, type of specimen, specimen collected by, and number of specimen(s) in the appropriate spaces on the Medical-Legal Specimen Control Record.
        (i) Have the applicant/employee sign the first "Received From" line;
        (ii) Sign the "Received By" and "Sealed By" lines, and record the date and time.
    d. Place the specimen in one zip-lock bag and the request form with the release form in a second zip-lock bag, and staple these together. Attach the Medical-Legal Specimen Control Record to this with a paper clip so that it may be removed when it needs to be signed.

APPLICANT/EMPLOYEE CONSENT FORMS

The following forms should be considered in obtaining an applicant's/employee's consent to employer alcohol and drug testing:

APPLICANT/EMPLOYEE CONSENT: FORM 1

   I, __(Name)__ , understand and agree that the physical examination I am about to receive includes a:

(   ) Blood test to detect the presence of alcohol/drugs in my system

(   ) Urine test to detect the presence of alcohol/drugs in my system

I understand that if I decline to sign this consent and decline to take the test, the physical examination will not be completed. The Human Resources Department will be notified and my application for employment will be rejected and/or my employment may be terminated. I understand that the test results and other medical information will be released only to authorized Company personnel for appropriate consideration.

   I have taken the following drugs, substances, or alcoholic beverages within the last 96 hours:

(   ) Sleeping pills _____

(   ) Diet pills _____

(   ) Pain relief pills _____

(   ) Cold tablets _____

(   ) Anti-malarial drugs _____

(   ) Prescription drugs _____

(   ) Any other medication or substance _____

(   ) Alcoholic beverages _____

I hereby (   ) consent

          (   ) refuse to consent

to the physical examination including the test(s) to detect the presence of alcohol/drugs in my system.

Date: _____   Signed: _____

Date: _____   Witness: _____

APPLICANT/EMPLOYEE CONSENT: FORM 2

I hereby voluntarily consent to allow the Company to collect urine and blood specimens from me for testing for alcohol, drugs, and controlled substances. Further, I give my consent for the release of the test results to the appropriate members of the Company's management. I understand that any positive result may preclude my employment.

_____   _____
Date   Signature

CHAIN OF CUSTODY FORM

The following form should be used to safeguard any urine, blood, hair, or other samples taken from an applicant/employee for alcohol or drug testing:

CHAIN OF CUSTODY FORM

Name: _____

Date/Time: _____

Employer: _____

PART I

I certify that I personally obtained the specimens enclosed in this envelope. These specimens were either in my personal possession or personally secured by me until passed on to the person whose signature appears on the line below mine:

Signature: _____

Date/Time: _____

PART II

I certify that I received this sealed envelope from the person whose name appears above mine and that it was either in my personal possession or personally secured by me until given to the person whose signature follows mine:

Signature: _____ Time: _____ Date: _____

Signature: _____ Time: _____ Date: _____

Signature: _____ Time: _____ Date: _____

Signature: _____ Time: _____ Date: _____

PART III

I certify that I received this sealed envelope from the person whose name appears above mine and that the seal showed no signs of having been broken. I opened the envelope and personally performed or supervised the performance of testing for alcohol or drug content.

Signature: _____

Date/Time: _____

EMPLOYEE REINSTATEMENT AGREEMENT FOR ALCOHOL OR
DRUG ABUSE

The following agreement should be considered where an employer desires to reinstate an employee who has been involved with alcohol or drug abuse:

EMPLOYEE REINSTATEMENT AGREEMENT FOR ALCOHOL OR DRUG ABUSE

It is hereby agreed as follows:

1. __(Employee's name)__ recognizes that the Company will conditionally reinstate __(Him or her)__ after he or she successfully completes a rehabilitation program at __(Name and location of rehabilitation program)__ ; provided the following conditions are met: _____(List conditions)_____

_____

_____

2. If within the next __(Describe time)__ , __(Employee's name)__ is unable to perform job duties due to alcohol or drug abuse, fails to continue an alcohol or drug rehabilitation program, or fails to meet the conditions set forth in "1" above, discipline up to and including termination may result.

3. I agree to cooperate in any additional alcohol or drug testing that the Company in its discretion deems appropriate during the __(Time period)__ immediately following my reinstatement, or discipline up to and including termination may result.

_____
(Date)

                                        _____
                                        (Employee)

                                        _____
                                        (Union Representative)

                                        _____
                                        (Employer)

ACQUIRED IMMUNE DEFICIENCY
SYNDROME (AIDS)

AIDS PRIVACY PRINCIPLES

Acquired immune deficiency syndrome (AIDS) is a disease that affects the body's immune system, rendering it vulnerable to infections and viruses. This disease has quickly become a significant employee privacy issue. It affects privacy interests present in association and lifestyle.

Constitutional employee privacy considerations that arise out of alcohol and drug testing are also applicable to AIDS testing. Mandatory AIDS blood testing infringes on the employee's privacy interest in disclosing non-job-related personal matters. Significant psychological trauma might accompany an erroneous diagnosis, and disclosure to others could have serious results. The employee's most intimate personal relationships could be affected by a positive test. A positive reading might be construed falsely to perceive an employee as a homosexual or a drug user. Through this, federal constitutional protections arising out of the First Amendment's associational rights,[4] the Fourth Amendment's guarantee against unreasonable searches,[5] and the Fifth Amendment's protection against self-incrimination[6] are impacted. State constitutional relief may also exist.

Federal and state FEP statutes may recognize AIDS as a protected handicap. While these statutes contain differences, their underlying intent is similar: that is, employees capable of working, without endangering themselves or others, should be allowed to do so regardless of a physical or medical condition which is, or is perceived to be, disabling. Likewise, tort and contract litigation theories may safeguard employee privacy interests relating to AIDS.

AIDS PROCEDURES

The following procedures should be considered in avoiding workplace AIDS conflicts:[7]

---

[4] U.S. Const. amend. I.

[5] U.S. Const. amend. IV.

[6] U.S. Const. amend. V.

[7] *See* Littler, Mendelson, Fastiff & Tichy, *Acquired Immune Deficiency Syndrome: The Problem of Accommodating Individual Rights with the Concerns of the Workplace,*

1. Consider initial planning for dealing with AIDS
2. Do not feel compelled to announce an AIDS policy, absent genuine workplace concerns, because:
   - Prematurely adopting an AIDS policy may lead employees to believe that the employer knows something that may create undue concern about an AIDS workplace risk
   - Not knowing the circumstances of how the AIDS issue will arise, it is difficult to make a premature commitment to any particular course of action
   - Unless some special risk of transmission exists, i.e., needle-stick injuries, the best policy is a case-by-case approach
3. Designate a small group of senior managers to deal with the AIDS issue, which should include people knowledgeable about the medical, human resource, and legal issues
4. Should the AIDS issue require action, institute employee AIDS education as the first step
5. Institute a reasonable AIDS policy that treats AIDS victims like those with any other degenerative, noninfectious disease, to minimize legal liability
6. Recognize that, given current technology, screening applicants or employees for AIDS may not be effective, because the most common blood serum AIDS antibody tests provide almost no useful information. In some states this testing is unlawful
7. Determine whether any federal, state, or local regulation would prohibit certain employee classes with infectious diseases from working in or near certain areas
8. Require an employee who is diagnosed with AIDS, or any other infectious or communicable disease:
   - To provide a physician's certificate outlining whether the employee should work under any particular restrictions
   - To provide a statement regarding whether the employee's being subject to exposure to common viruses

in The 1987 Employer 0, 0–23 to 0–24 (1987). Littler, Mendelson, Fastiff & Tichy prepare this publication on an annual basis for Business Laws, Inc. of 8228 Mayfield Road in Chesterland, Ohio 44026; telephone (216) 729-7996. This publication is an excellent reference source for human resource professionals and attorneys as an annual update of employment laws.

For a further discussion of AIDS in the workplace, *see* AIDS and the Law ch. 3 (W.H.L. Dornette ed., John Wiley & Sons 1987).

carried by other workers might pose an imminent and substantial risk to his or her health

9. If the physician requires that work or exposure to others be restricted, make efforts to reasonably accommodate the AIDS-afflicted employee by:
   - A job redefinition
   - Transfer
   - Consultation with the physician attending a pregnant employee might also be indicated

10. If the physician imposes no restrictions, and assuming that there are no other health or safety restrictions imposed by law with respect to the employee, permit the employee with AIDS to continue working in his or her job

11. Advise employees, based on the consensus of medical opinion, that there is no risk of contracting AIDS in a normal workplace environment

12. If an employee refuses to work with an AIDS victim, follow alternative courses, such as:
    - The employee may be treated in accordance with counseling or progressive discipline procedures
    - Reference may be made to employer policies regarding insubordination or harassment of employees who are members of a protected class
    - The employer may wish to avail itself of the conciliation and remedial powers of a FEP agency to resolve the situation

13. Treat AIDS victims who, by virtue of their illness, no longer are able to work, the same as any employee who has a long-term, debilitating disease

14. Respect privacy rights and statutory rights to medical information confidentiality of AIDS-afflicted employees, in that disclosing that an employee has AIDS beyond those individuals with a need to know, can lead to:
    - Costly litigation
    - Increased anxiety among co-employees

AIDS POLICIES

The following should be considered where an employer determines that it is appropriate to address the AIDS issue:

AIDS POLICY

Section 1. Purpose. The Company will deal with acquired immune deficiency syndrome (AIDS) in a humanitarian and nondiscriminatory fashion, while assuring the safety and health of all employees. All employees will be trained to understand AIDS.

Section 2. Nondiscrimination. The Company is committed to a responsible policy of nondiscrimination regarding AIDS. An employee afflicted with AIDS will be treated the same as any other employee suffering from a long-term disability.

Section 3. Confidentiality. The Company will respect the confidentiality of all employees afflicted with AIDS.

Section 4. Employment. The Company will employ applicants or employees who have AIDS or are suspected of having AIDS, so long as these persons remain qualified to perform their jobs. Some exceptions or deviations to this policy may be necessary for certain positions, but the Company will employ AIDS patients, while at the same time preserving the safety and morale of all its employees. According to the best medical evidence available to date, casual workplace contact with employees who have AIDS, or who have been exposed to the AIDS virus, will not result in the transmission of AIDS to others.

Section 5. Policy Updates. The Company will remain current regarding the latest medical knowledge pertaining to this disease. Should it subsequently appear that this policy's implementation may present a danger to employees, the Company will make appropriate policy revisions.

Health Care Employer's AIDS Policy

For health care employers, the following policy should be considered in that it does not single AIDS out specifically, but deals with it in an overall infectious disease control policy to minimize employee overreaction:

AIDS POLICY

Section 1. Policy. It is the Company's policy to establish procedures regarding infectious disease control and to present guidelines for the education, counseling, and management related to employees and program participants.

Section 2. Education and Training. Education and training shall be provided to employees regarding infectious diseases and made available to all program participants. All employees will receive education and training regarding infectious diseases to implement and follow the Center for Disease Control's (CDC's) universal precautions in all Company programs and offices. Program participant training in areas involving personal hygiene, sexuality, and first aid will incorporate information on infectious disease.

Initial training and yearly update trainings are mandatory for all employees. Employees will attend a basic education session on infectious diseases which will occur as needed but at least annually. This will be an orientation requirement. Additional training or counseling will be conducted to meet specific needs of employees and to disseminate updated information as necessary. All employees will receive training regarding death and dying. A health services specialist will be designated and trained to function as the trainer, and to be responsible for the continual dissemination of accurate and updated information on infectious diseases.

Section 3. Precautionary Guidelines. The Company will implement precautionary guidelines in its programs and offices to prevent the transmission of infectious diseases in those work settings where program participant care, treatment, and services are provided.

Section 4. Discrimination and Confidentiality. No employee or program participant shall be discriminated against in the provision of services or hiring because of the presence of an infectious disease. His/her confidentiality shall not be breached regarding this matter, except as may be strictly required under applicable legislative, regulatory, or court requirements.

Program participants and employees have the right to privacy and individual human dignity. Disciplinary action, up to and including termination, will be taken for any employee disclosing confidential information. Information regarding an individual's diagnosis and health will be communicated only when a clear "need-to-know" is established based on the program's needs.

Section 5. Infected Employees. Infected employees will not routinely be relieved of assignments or restricted from work unless they have an illness for which a restriction would be warranted. Infected employees will be evaluated on an individual basis, considering the health status of the employee and the nature of the employee's responsibilities. As a normal practice, infected employees will maintain their assigned duties. However, based on individual circumstances associated with a given case, reassignment may be requested or recommended. These decisions are to be made in consultation with the affected employee and the employee's physician.

Section 6. Medical Services. As long as community medical services are sufficient, available, and appropriate to meet the needs of the program participants with infectious disease, the Company will continue to provide services.

Section 7. Infectious Diseases' Procedures. The following infectious disease will be followed:

a. Information on infectious diseases shall be made available to all employees and program participants.

b. Education and training regarding infectious diseases shall be provided to both employees and program participants. The education program should include at least the following:

   (1) What is an Infectious Disease;
   (2) How infectious diseases affect the immune system;
   (3) Who is at risk;
   (4) Methods of transmission;
   (5) How to prevent getting and transmitting infectious diseases;
   (6) General symptoms;
   (7) How to obtain additional information;
   (8) Issues of death and dying; and
   (9) Confidentiality.

c. All employees will receive a copy of this policy as part of their initial training.

d. In addition, the Center for Disease Control's (CDC's) *universal precautions* shall be instituted in every program and office of the Company in that persons can significantly reduce their risk of exposure to infectious diseases if hygiene recommendations are implemented. These include emphasis on a clean environment and careful personal hygiene. Due to the possibility of transmitting an infectious disease prenatally, pregnant and child-bearing age employees should be especially familiar with the universal precautions. The following hygiene procedures shall be implemented in all Company programs and offices:

   1. Scrupulous personal hygiene must be followed by employees and program participants at all times. FREQUENT, CAREFUL HANDWASHING USING PLENTY OF SOAP AND WATER SHALL BE CARRIED OUT.
   2. Personal toiletry items shall not be shared. Specifically this includes razors, towels, washcloths, toothbrushes, nail clippers, soap, and so forth.
   3. Discourage all program participants from placing others fingers in their mouths or their fingers into other's mouths.
   4. Cover open breaks (lesions) in the skin.
   5. Thoroughly clean with soap and water or discard items soiled by blood or body fluids. All blood-soiled items such as sanitary napkins should be double bagged as an appropriate protection when being discarded.
   6. Disinfect blood contaminated objects if this can be done without

damaging the contaminated surface. If the contaminated object cannot be cleaned without damaging the surface, the object should be discarded. The most commonly suggested disinfectant is a solution of sodium hypochlorite (household bleach) at a recommended strength of one and one-half cups of bleach per gallon of water. The solution should be made fresh daily and used to clean areas that have been soiled with blood or body fluids. Other appropriate disinfectants include alcohol, peroxide, and Lysol.

7. The following protective wear is available and shall be utilized as necessary to minimize the risks of infection:

    a. Gloves: Should be worn when handling urine specimens, blood soiled items, body fluids, excretions, and secretions, as well as surfaces, materials, and objects exposed to them.

    b. Gowns/Aprons: Should be worn when clothing may be soiled with body fluids, blood, secretions, or excretions.

    c. Masks/Protective Eyewear/Face Shields: Should be worn when face area may be splashed with body fluids, blood, secretions, or excretions, as in implementing some dental hygiene programs.

8. Extraordinary care must be taken to avoid accidental wounds from sharp instruments and needles.

9. To minimize the need for emergency direct mouth-to-mouth resuscitation, mouth pieces should be strategically located and available for use.

10. Routine cleaning of dishes, eating utensils, and toilet facilities is adequate to eliminate the risk of disease transmission. Dishes and eating utensils may be washed in a dishwasher or by hand at normal water temperature (110 degrees Fahrenheit) without the use of any special disinfectant. They do not need to be washed separately. Disposable gloves should be used if dishes are soiled with blood or saliva.

11. Each program participant's clothing, towels, and bed linens should be laundered separately. Laundry items contaminated with blood or body fluids should be handled with gloves and stored and washed separately.

12. Employees and program participants are encouraged to avoid high risk behaviors which include the exchange of blood or body fluids.

6

WORKPLACE INFORMATION COLLECTION AND DISTRIBUTION

Information collection continues at the workplace after an employee is hired. Generally, employer workplace information collection involves updating, maintaining, and using information that has already been obtained, or procuring new information necessitated by workplace requirements.

At times, surreptitious methods may be used to collect workplace information that affects employee privacy interests arising out of speech, beliefs, and associations. Occasionally, employees or outside third parties may seek to solicit or distribute information at the workplace. Depending upon the employer, various restrictions may be placed on these information solicitation and distribution activities. This chapter reviews workplace information collection and distribution procedures that arise out of searches, monitoring, and surveillance, along with literature solicitation and distribution.

SEARCHES

SEARCH PRIVACY PRINCIPLES

Employer security problems have broadened from concerns over property and information theft to safeguarding the workplace from alcohol and drug abuse. Searches or potential searches can create significant privacy problems for employers by uncovering information that the employee has not voluntarily revealed and that may not be job-related. Employees who are stopped and searched may assert several claims against employers involving invasion of privacy, defamation, false imprisonment, false arrest, malicious prosecution, intentional infliction of emotional distress, and constitutional right infringement.

False imprisonment arises when employers detain employees, even briefly, to search their bags, cases, purses, or person through a total restraint on the freedom to move that is against the employee's will. Generally, the employee must be aware of the restraint. Merely stopping an employee is not a total restraint. The restraint, however, need not be lengthy or physically confining; that is, the employee need not be locked in a room. Advising an employee not to leave may be a sufficient restraint. Awareness is not necessary where substantial damages result from the confinement. Where an employee remains free to leave despite being asked questions or being accompanied to or from work during an investigation, no false imprisonment occurs.

Liability can be incurred through a false arrest for theft brought about by some employer affirmative direction, persuasion, request, or voluntary participation. Generally, the employer does not incur potential false arrest liability until it actually causes the arrest of an employee.

The employer does not commit a false arrest by providing truthful information to law enforcement authorities and allowing them to make a determination. Where information given to police is known to be false, and the employer insists on arrest, then the employer may be liable for false arrest. Probable cause for an arrest and detention is a valid defense to a false arrest or imprisonment claim. *Probable cause* means having more evidence for than against the arrest, such as a good faith, reasonable belief in the validity of the arrest and detention. A signed, uncoerced statement admitting employee responsibility may protect an employer from liability.

To establish malicious prosecution, an employee generally must show that a false accusation by the employer has been made, with knowledge of the statement's falsity or a reckless disregard for its truth, that causes arrest, confinement, or other damages to the person accused. This may arise in search situations when, for example, theft is alleged and the employer does more than discipline, causing a meritless criminal prosecution to be instituted.

Defamation consists of libel or slander. It requires a showing of accusation of a crime, or some other act that would bring disrepute to the employee, that is made falsely or with reckless disregard for its truth and is communicated to others orally or in writing. Defamation liability may arise out of workplace search situations when the employer accuses an employee of theft and communicates this accusation to others not entitled to this information. Should the employer's search lead to an accusation causing employee emotional upset with serious physical manifestations, a claim for intentional infliction of emotional distress maybe made.

SEARCH PROCEDURES

Search Considerations

In developing workplace search procedures, the following should be considered:

1. Applications should provide that employees agree to employer searches
2. The search procedure and policy should be communicated and explained to all employees
3. Employees should be informed that the purpose of the search is to deter theft and that the employee being searched is not under suspicion
4. Employees should not be selected for searches randomly, arbitrarily, capriciously, or discriminatorily

Human Resource Staff Theft Investigations

In investigating alleged workplace thefts, the human resource staff should consider the following:[1]

1. Upon learning of theft allegations:
   - Notify and consult with legal counsel
   - Structure the theft investigation to maximize the likelihood that the attorney-client and the attorney work product privileges apply
   - Consider whether legal counsel should participate in the investigation
2. Evaluate the need for special expertise in theft situations involving:

---

[1] See Murphy, *Investigating, Handling, and Protecting Against Employee Theft and Dishonesty*, in J. Kauff, Employment Problems in the Workplace 22-23 (1986).

- Time mischarging, purchasing fraud, travel pay fraud, and so forth, where an accountant may need to be involved
- Theft of computer services, where a computer expert may be necessary

3. Establish the alleged theft's essentials regarding:
   - By whom
   - Against whom
   - Persons involved
   - Nature of the improper act
   - When it occurred

4. Determine whether to inform the suspected employee of the investigation and suspend him or her pending the outcome, or leave the employee at the workplace to obtain additional evidence of any wrongdoing

5. Investigation procedures:
   - Interview all potential witnesses, including employees and outside third parties
   - Consider obtaining signed statements from persons who may later take a position adverse to the employer
   - Examine all pertinent records and documents
   - Avoid group interviews
   - Be impartial and take care not to convey a prosecutorial image
   - Take thorough, detailed, and exact notes by:
     — Using the witness's language
     — Including proper names, job titles, salary grades, and reporting relationships for persons interviewed and mentioned
     — Reviewing notes with the person interviewed to fill gaps or make necessary corrections

SEARCH POLICY

To inform employees of the employer's right to conduct workplace searches, the following policy and/or notice should be considered:

SEARCH POLICY

The Company reserves the right to question any person entering and leaving its property and to inspect any person, locker, vehicle, package, purse, handbag, briefcase, lunchbox, or other possessions carried to, on, and from its property. This includes all of the Company's employees.

MONITORING

MONITORING PRIVACY PRINCIPLES

Monitoring involves using mechanical or electronic devices to obtain workplace employee information. Computer, telephone, and video technology are the most common types of workplace monitoring.

Workplace monitoring's extent is unknown because it is done without employee awareness. Any time computers or telephones are used in the workplace, there is monitoring potential. Federal and state statutes regulate certain workplace monitoring. Employers may subject themselves to employee privacy claims when monitoring devices are knowingly used to obtain nonjob-related information that may reveal speech, belief, and associational interests. Invasion of privacy, defamation, or public policy violations could be alleged.

MONITORING PROCEDURES

General Monitoring Considerations

Before undertaking monitoring, the employer should:[2]

1. Review the applicability of any federal or state statutes regulating the proposed monitoring
2. Ensure that the monitoring is job-related
3. Clearly notify employees that job performance may be subject to monitoring
4. As a condition of employment, obtain the employee's written consent to monitoring job performance
5. Disclose to employees what mechanical or electronic devices may be used for monitoring job performance
6. Disclose to employees when, where, and how these mechanical or electronic devices may be used for monitoring job performance
7. Consider the fairness of work performance standards:
    - Do they fairly reflect the particular work force's abilities?

[2] Office of Technology Assessment, The Electronic Supervisor: New Technology, New Tensions 29, 38 (1987).

- Will they create stress for many employees?
- Do they account for recurring system difficulties and other workplace problems?
- Do they include quality as well as quantity goals?
- Do they represent a fair day's pay for a fair day's work?
- Do employees share in productivity gains achieved through new technology?

8. Consider the fairness of the measurement process:
   - Do employees know and understand how the measurements are being done?
   - Can the measurement system be defeated, impairing morale of those willing to follow the rules?
   - Do employees receive statistics on performance directly and in time to affect their work rate?
   - Is the relationship between quality and quantity communicated by supervisors when discussing problems with performance?
   - Do supervisors communicate clearly that they are taking system/workplace problems into account?
   - Are group rather than individual rates used when this approach is more equitable?
   - Is there a formal complaint process for contesting how work data is used?

9. Consider the fairness in applying the measurements to performance evaluations:
   - Are there meaningful recognition programs for superior performance?
   - Is work quantity only one of a well-rounded and objective set of evaluation criteria?
   - Does the employee see and participate in the performance evaluation?
   - Is there an appeal process from the supervisor's performance evaluation?
   - Is there a performance-planning system to identify and help performance problems?

Monitoring Uses

Workplace monitoring may be used to measure and document employee transactions involving:

1. Planning and scheduling personnel and equipment
2. Evaluating employee performance and personnel decisions concerning promotion, retraining, termination, and so forth
3. Increasing productivity by providing feedback on speed, work pacing, and so forth
4. Providing security for employer property, including intellectual property and personnel records
5. Investigating incidents of misconduct, crime, or human error
6. Increasing employer control, discouraging union organizing activities, identifying dissidents, and so forth

MONITORING POLICIES

Work Performance Monitoring

The following policy should be considered regarding workplace monitoring:

WORK PERFORMANCE MONITORING

The Company may periodically monitor or review employee work performance through the use of mechanical or electronic devices. Among the mechanical or electronic devices that the Company may use are telephone monitoring, transponders, beepers, pen registers, touch-tone decoders, diodes, and so forth. These may be used to limit personal calls at the workplace, review driver routes, investigate workplace problems, and so forth.

Work Performance Monitoring:
Employee Authorization

Where workplace monitoring is used, the following employee authorization should be considered:

WORK PERFORMANCE MONITORING: EMPLOYEE AUTHORIZATION

As an employment condition, I understand that the Company may periodically monitor or review my work performance by using mechanical or electronic devices. Among the devices that the Company may use are telephone monitoring, transponders, beepers, pen registers, touch-tone decoders, and diodes. To this work performance monitoring, I expressly consent.

_____
Employee Signature

_____
Date

SURVEILLANCE

Unlike monitoring, surveillance generally involves physical observation of employees without their knowledge. Surveillance may be done by observation, extraction, or reproduction. Observational surveillance involves viewing the employee at the workplace, although the employee may not be aware of this. Surveillance by extraction generally involves employee information collection through questionable testing, such as by a polygraph examination, honesty testing, and so forth. Reproduction surveillance generally involves employee information collection through photographic, recording, or other similar devices.

Employers use surveillance for various purposes. These purposes may include:

1. Determining union organization activity extent
2. General workplace surveillance for job performance purposes
3. Manipulating employees
4. Photographing employees
5. Electronic surveillance.

SURVEILLANCE PROCEDURES

Before undertaking surveillance, the employer should:

1. Review the applicability of any federal or state statutes regulating the proposed surveillance
2. Ensure that the surveillance is job-related
3. Clearly notify employees that their job performance may be subject to surveillance
4. As a condition of employment, obtain the employee's written consent to job performance surveillance
5. Disclose to employees what mechanical, electronic, or other devices may be used for job performance surveillance
6. Disclose to employees when, where, and how these mechanical, electronic, or other devices may be used for job performance surveillance

SURVEILLANCE POLICIES

Work Performance Surveillance Policy

The following policy should be considered regarding workplace surveillance:

WORK PERFORMANCE SURVEILLANCE POLICY

The Company may periodically monitor, survey, or review employee work performance through the use of mechanical, electronic, or other methods, which may include photographing, observation, telephone monitoring, transponders, beepers, pen registers, touch-tone decoder, diodes, and so forth.

Work Performance Surveillance:
Employee Authorization

Where workplace surveillance is used, the following employee authorization should be considered:

WORK PERFORMANCE SURVEILLANCE: EMPLOYEE AUTHORIZATION

As an employment condition, I understand that the Company may periodically survey, monitor, or review my work performance by using mechanical, electronic, or other methods. To this work performance surveillance, I expressly consent.

_____
Employee Signature

_____
Date

LITERATURE SOLICITATION
AND DISTRIBUTION

LITERATURE SOLICITATION AND DISTRIBUTION
PRIVACY PRINCIPLES

Employee privacy is affected through an employer's regulation of workplace literature solicitation and distribution. This regulation or restriction curtails certain aspects of employee constitutional speech, association, and right to information. Regulation may cause employees to refrain from exercising union organizational rights under federal and state labor relations statutes.

These employee privacy interests normally arise when literature is brought into or distributed at the workplace by employees or third parties. This may extend to prohibiting the reading of "adult" literature, soliciting donations for a charitable organization during lunch periods, and so forth.

LITERATURE SOLICITATION AND
DISTRIBUTION PROCEDURES

Federal and state labor relations boards have set certain presumptions regarding employer rules regulating union solicitation and distribution. Employer literature solicitation and distribution rules are generally valid absent a showing of the employer's antiunion animus or discrimination. It is presumptively valid for an employer to promulgate a rule prohibiting:

1. Union solicitation by employees in work areas during working time
2. Solicitation by employees during nonworking time, even if on employer property
3. Literature distribution by employees in work areas at any time
4. Literature distribution by employees in nonwork areas during nonwork time

LITERATURE SOLICITATION AND DISTRIBUTION POLICIES

The following policies should be considered regarding literature solicitation and distribution:

LITERATURE SOLICITATION AND DISTRIBUTION POLICY No. 1

Solicitation, distribution of literature, or trespassing by nonemployees on these premises are prohibited.

LITERATURE SOLICITATION AND DISTRIBUTION POLICY No. 2

Distribution of advertising material, handbills, or other literature in working areas of this plant is prohibited at any time,

LITERATURE SOLICITATION AND DISTRIBUTION POLICY No. 3

Solicitation by an employee of another employee is prohibited while either the person doing the soliciting or the person being solicited is on working time. Working time is the period when an employee is required to perform his or her job duties.

7

PERSONAL WORKPLACE
PRIVACY CONCERNS

Workplace concerns affecting employee privacy interests generally involve exercising certain duties, choices, or rights along with the employer's restriction or accommodation of these. Privacy interests present in speech, beliefs, associations, and lifestyles may be affected at the workplace. This chapter reviews personal workplace privacy concerns that may arise out of jury or witness duty, voting time, whistleblowing, dress and grooming codes, spousal policies, nepotism, third-party representation, performance evaluations, religious accommodation, privacy misconduct, sexual harassment, and restrictive covenants.

JURY OR WITNESS DUTY

JURY OR WITNESS DUTY PRIVACY PRINCIPLES

Jury or witness responsibilities are employee privacy interests involving speech, beliefs, and association concerns that extend to general societal obligations with which an employer cannot interfere. A strong public policy implicit in federal and state constitutions, statutes, and decisional law encourages jury service. Statutory protections for this privacy interest generally entitle an employee to take time off for jury duty or for a court appearance as a witness when reasonable notice is given to the employer. The employer is prohibited from terminating or discriminating against an employee for taking time off for this purpose.

221

JURY OR WITNESS DUTY PROCEDURES

In developing jury or witness duty procedures, the following should be considered:

1. Review federal and state statutes for any requirements regarding time off, payment, and so forth
2. Proof of jury or witness duty should be presented
3. Requests for jury duty should be made in advance so as not to interfere unnecessarily with employer staffing requirements

JURY OR WITNESS DUTY POLICY

The following policy should be considered regarding employees who are confronted with jury or witness duty obligations:

JURY OR WITNESS DUTY POLICY

Upon receiving a summons to report for jury or witness duty, an employee shall, on his or her next working day, present the summons to his or her immediate superior. The employee shall be excused from employment for the day or days required in serving as a juror or witness in any court created by the United States or the State of __(State's name)__ . This shall be considered an excused absence. Full-time employees shall be entitled to their usual compensation less any fee or compensation received from serving as jurors or witnesses upon written presentation to the Company.

VOTING TIME

VOTING TIME PRIVACY PRINCIPLES

Voting is a general societal obligation to which employee privacy interests extend. It affects speech, beliefs, and associational privacy interests regarding political choices. A strong public policy implicit in federal and state constitutions, statutes, and decisional law encourages voting. Some states require that an employee be given time off to vote.

VOTING TIME PROCEDURES

In developing voting time procedures, the following should be considered:

1. Applicable federal and state statutes should be reviewed for any requirements regarding time off, payment, and so forth
2. Requests for voting time should be made in advance of the election date so as not to interfere unnecessarily with employer requirements
3. Proof that voting time was used by the employee
4. Voter registration verification, by having the employee sign an authorization-to-vote form indicating:
   • That the employee is an eligible registered voter for the subject election
   • That falsification may result in employee discipline up to and including termination

VOTING TIME POLICY

The following policy should be considered regarding employees who desire to vote during working time:

VOTING TIME POLICY

Section 1. Time Off. Company employees are entitled to vote at general, primary, or presidential primary elections. When registered voter-employees do not have sufficient time outside of regular working hours to vote, they may take off so much working time as will, when added to their voting time outside their working hours, enable them to vote. Employees shall be allowed time off for voting only at the beginning or end of their regular working shifts, whichever allows them the most free time for voting and the least time off from their regular working shift, unless otherwise mutually agreed. Employees who are election officers may absent themselves from employment on election day without being subject to demotion, suspension, or termination; provided sufficient advance notice is given to the Company.

Section 2. Compensation. Employees may take off so much time as will enable them to vote, but not more than two hours of which shall be without loss of pay.

Section 3. Time-off Notice. If an employee knows or has reason to believe that time off is needed to vote, he or she must give the Company at least five working days' notice that time off is desired for voting.

WHISTLEBLOWING

WHISTLEBLOWING PRIVACY PRINCIPLES

Related to employee privacy speech, belief, and associational interests is an employee's discipline or termination arising out of a whistleblowing incident. *Whistleblowing* involves required participation or reporting of unlawful and/or improper conduct by the employer or a fellow employee to the employer or to government authorities. Federal and state statutes increasingly protect whistleblowing.

WHISTLEBLOWING PROCEDURES

In developing whistleblowing procedures, the following should be considered:

1. Applicable federal and state statutes protecting whistleblowing
2. Internal complaint procedures for resolving whistleblowing incidents
3. Offering protection for legitimate whistleblowing complaints
4. Prohibiting retaliation for legitimate whistleblowing complaints

WHISTLEBLOWING PROTECTION POLICY

The following policy should be considered regarding whistleblowing:

WHISTLEBLOWING PROTECTION POLICY

Section 1.   Purpose.   It is the Company's policy to follow and enforce all federal, state, and local laws applicable to it and to require its employees to do likewise. Every employee has the responsibility to assist in implementing this policy.

Section 2.   Reporting Company Violations.   A violation of this policy should be reported to an employee's immediate supervisor in writing and signed by the employee. However, if that is not practical, a written statement, signed and dated, should be submitted by the employee to the Director of Human Resources so that an investigation may be undertaken.

Section 3.   No Retaliation for Filing Complaints.   There will be no retaliation by the Company or any of its employees against any employee who makes a good faith report pursuant to this policy, even if after investigation it is determined that there has not been a violation.

Section 4.   Corrective Action.   It is the responsibility of the Company to correct or prevent violations of federal, state, and local laws applicable to it. This is a legal obligation. A violation can cause the Company and its employees to be subjected to publicity leading to an adverse image in the eyes of the public, customers, and the government.

Section 5.   Violation of This Policy.   The procedures outlined herein must be followed before any employee reports alleged violations to any news medium, government agency, and so forth. Employee complaints that do not follow this procedure constitute a policy violation. Adhering to this policy is an employment condition. The Company should have the opportunity to conduct the investigation first, and each employee should ensure that the Company can undertake this investigation.

DRESS AND GROOMING CODES

DRESS AND GROOMING CODE PRIVACY PRINCIPLES

Employer dress rules in some way always inhibit or restrict the employee's personal freedom. These rules may designate the clothing type or uniform that must be worn by employees or that may not be worn at the workplace. Personal taste or style may be one of the more significant employee privacy interests that an employer seeks to affect or regulate at the workplace. It deals directly with speech, belief, and lifestyle privacy interests.

Dress and grooming standards may be imposed by the employer as part of health and safety requirements, customer relations, image, or business type. They may also arise informally through employee peer pressure; the workplace norm among employees becomes an unofficial dress and grooming standard that they have established for themselves over a given time period, to which new employees must conform or be ostracized.

Despite an employer's right to set these policies, certain employee privacy interests may be adversely affected. These primarily involve violations of federal and state FEP statutes.

DRESS AND GROOMING CODE PROCEDURES

The following should be considered regarding dress and grooming codes:

1. Health and safety requirements
2. Customer relations
3. Employer image
4. Business type
5. Job-relatedness

DRESS AND GROOMING CODE POLICY

The following policy should be considered concerning dress and grooming:

DRESS AND GROOMING CODE POLICY

While at the workplace, this Company acknowledges the employee's right to dress and groom as he or she chooses, unless the employee's dress or grooming has an adverse effect on the Company's business or the employee's health and safety.

SPOUSAL POLICIES

SPOUSAL PRIVACY PRINCIPLES

Employer spousal policies may restrict or deny employment with the same employer because one is or becomes a husband or wife. Marriage or subsequent marriage may result in a failure to hire, transfer to another department, demotion, or termination.

As a privacy interest, spousal policies affect associational considerations. One is restrained or penalized for taking part in life's basic relationship of husband and wife. However, these policies have generally been permitted as a reasonable employer method of eliminating possible employee conflicts or favoritism that may grow out of or originate in the husband-and-wife relationship. Spousal policies are generally impacted by federal and state FEP statutes, although constitutional claims may also be asserted.

SPOUSAL PROCEDURES

In developing spousal procedures, the following should be considered to avoid conflict:

1. Equal application to both sexes
2. Neutral effect on both spouses
3. Confidentiality considerations
4. Job-relatedness by evaluating that:
   - Spouses may support one another
   - The marital relationship may generate emotional problems detrimental to job performance
   - Favoritism may exist between spouses
   - A spouse in a supervisory position over the other spouse maybe less inclined to recognize or deal with unsatisfactory job performance

SPOUSAL EMPLOYMENT POLICY

The following policy should be considered concerning spousal employment:

SPOUSAL EMPLOYMENT POLICY

Each employee is, if otherwise qualified, entitled to work with that employee's spouse. The Company does not discriminate against an applicant or an employee regarding working conditions, workplace assignment, or other employment privileges because that applicant's or employee's spouse is also a Company employee. However, this does not apply to employment of the spouse of a person who has the responsibility to hire, fire, or to conduct performance evaluations of the position involved. That spouse may not be hired, may be transferred, or may be terminated.

NEPOTISM

NEPOTISM PRIVACY PRINCIPLES

Nepotism is the practice of favoring relatives over others. With respect to employee privacy interests, a nepotism policy affects associational considerations prohibiting or restricting working relationships with relatives, as do spousal policies. Nepotism policies have generally been permitted as a reasonable employer method of minimizing employee conflict or favoritism arising out of close family relations. These policies are usually challenged under federal and state FEP statutes.

NEPOTISM PROCEDURES

In developing nepotism procedures, the following should be considered:

1. Applicable federal and state statutes
2. Neutral effect on all national origins
3. Job-relatedness
4. Confidentiality considerations

NEPOTISM POLICY

The following policy should be considered regarding nepotism:

NEPOTISM POLICY

Section 1. Family Member Employment. The Company considers it an unlawful employment practice regarding a member of an individual's family working or who has worked for the Company to:

a. Refuse to hire or employ that individual;
b. Bar or terminate from employment that individual; or
c. Discriminate against that individual in compensation or in terms, conditions, or privileges of employment.

Section 2. Conflict of Interest. The Company is not required to hire or continue in employment an individual if it:

a. Would place the individual in a position of exercising supervisory, appointment, or grievance adjustment authority over a member of the individual's family, or in a position of being subject to the authority that a member of the individual's family exercises; or
b. Would cause the Company to disregard a bona fide occupational requirement reasonably necessary to the normal operation of the Company's business.

Section 3. Member of an Individual's Family. *Member of an individual's family* includes wife, husband, son, daughter, mother, father, brother, brother-in-law, sister, sister-in-law, son-in-law, daughter-in-law, mother-in-law, father-in-law, aunt, uncle, niece, nephew, stepparent, or stepchild of the individual.

THIRD-PARTY REPRESENTATION

THIRD-PARTY REPRESENTATION PRIVACY PRINCIPLES

The right to representation at investigatory interviews for union and nonunion employees is an important privacy concept. This concept allows an employee a limited opportunity to safeguard certain workplace privacy interests when discipline or termination situations arise. It protects employee privacy interests present in speech, beliefs, information, association, and lifestyles.

Private and public sector employees have a qualified right to union representation during employer-initiated investigatory interviews. The right arises when the employee reasonably believes the investigation will result in disciplinary action, but only if the employee specifically requests union representation.

When an employee demands union representation, the employer has two alternatives. First, the investigation may be pursued without an interview. Second, union representation may be allowed, but the union representative's participation may be restricted. There is no obligation to bargain with the union at the interview, and the employer may insist upon hearing only the employee's version. A collateral right has been suggested for nonunion private and public sector employees.

THIRD-PARTY REPRESENTATION PROCEDURES

In dealing with third-party representation rights, the following should be considered:[1]

1. An investigatory interview is a meeting in which the employee is asked questions about employee misconduct and the employee reasonably believes that this interview will result in his or her being disciplined.
2. The employee must affirmatively request representation to invoke his or her rights.
3. The employee's request can be made before the interview or at any time during the interview.
4. There is no obligation that the employer advise the employee of his or her right to request representation.

[1] See American Hospital Association, The Wrongful Discharge of Employees in the Health Care Industry 102–103 (1987).

5. Upon the employee's timely request, the employer should disclose the subject matter to the employee prior to the investigatory interview, and permit the employee to consult privately with a representative if he or she so requests.

6. The employer can insist that the representative remain silent until the employee gives his or her own account of the incident, but the employer cannot insist that the representative be silent for the entire investigatory interview.

7. The representative can assist the employee and clarify any misconceptions that may arise, but the employer can insist on hearing only the employee's account.

8. The representative does not have to be brought in if the employee is simply disciplined without the occurrence of any interrogation or questioning, but if the employer wants to question the employee in the meeting after imposing the discipline, the employee can request the presence of the representative.

9. If an employee requests a representative, the employer may decide not to have any interview whatsoever, and may simply proceed with the investigation through other means.

THIRD-PARTY REPRESENTATION POLICIES

Third-Party Representation Policy (Union Employer)

The following policy should be considered by union employers in dealing with requests for representatives at investigatory interviews:

THIRD-PARTY REPRESENTATION POLICY
(UNION EMPLOYER)

Prior to any discipline, the Union shall be given an opportunity to discuss the matter with the Company. If an Employee who suspects discipline so requests, he or she shall be permitted to talk privately with one Union Representative before being interviewed by the Company.

A member of the bargaining unit who is requested to meet with a manager or supervisor for the purpose of imposing disciplinary action shall be entitled to be accompanied by a Union representative. The employee shall receive reasonable prior notice of the topics to be discussed.

Third-Party Representation: Nonunion Employer

The following policy should be considered by nonunion employers in dealing with requests for representatives at investigatory interviews:

THIRD-PARTY REPRESENTATION POLICY
(NONUNION EMPLOYER)

An employee who is requested to meet with a manager or supervisor for the purpose of imposing disciplinary action shall be entitled to be accompanied by another employee of his or her choosing. The employee shall receive reasonable prior notice of the topics to be discussed.

PERFORMANCE EVALUATIONS

PERFORMANCE EVALUATION PRIVACY PRINCIPLES

Employee privacy interests that are present in performance evaluations require that such evaluations be undertaken, collected, used, maintained, and disclosed with the utmost care. These records influence employee advancement, compensation, and assignment. Because of this information's sensitivity, confidentiality must be preserved by the employer. Performance evaluations also must be accurately completed.

Failure to preserve performance evaluation confidentiality may result in employer liability arising out of wrongful information disclosure. Maintenance of inaccurate information may result in suits for invasion of privacy, when a broad public disclosure of private facts occurs; defamation; intentional infliction of emotional distress, if conduct is outrageous; negligent maintenance or disclosure of employment records; or public policy violations. Contractual breaches may also arise where employment handbooks and collective bargaining agreements exist.

PERFORMANCE EVALUATION PROCEDURES

Performance Evaluation Purposes

Accurate and regular employee job performance evaluation is important, and the following should be considered:

1. Performance evaluations should be conducted annually.
2. Performance evaluations should review:
   - Job knowledge
   - Work quality
   - Work quantity
   - Initiative
   - Adaptability
   - Dependability
   - Cooperation
   - Improvement areas
   - Punctuality
   - Attendance

3. The performance evaluation should allow the employer to identify areas where the employee is performing adequately and areas where the employee needs to improve.

4. The performance evaluation may be used to determine promotion, layoff, or termination.

Performance Evaluation Interview

A performance evaluation interview should be conducted in a comfortable setting and should place the employee at ease. It should not be confused with a disciplinary interview. Prior to the interview, the following should be undertaken:[2]

1. Schedule the meeting sufficiently in advance to allow everyone time to prepare

2. Arrange a location that provides privacy and freedom from interruptions

3. Inform the employee of the meeting

4. Compile the employee's last performance evaluation, job description, and the employer's current salary guidelines

5. Allow sufficient time for the interview

6. Choose an appropriate time that allows an opportunity to do further follow-up with the employee before the day is over

7. Become familiar with the employee's personality and how he or she is likely to react to the interview

8. During the interview:
   - Discuss the employee's typical performance and do not overemphasize recent or isolated events
   - Discuss all factors evaluated rather than scrutinizing one or two in particular
   - Maintain consistency and objectivity
   - Do not be overly swayed by previous performance evaluations
   - Discuss with the employee plans for future development and identify methods for improving in deficient areas and for gaining additional skills

9. Take follow-up steps after the discussion by:

---

[2] See Dreesen, *The Increasing Importance of Effective Performance Appraisals*, 4 Special Focus 3, 4 (Oct. 1987).

- Having the employee acknowledge the review by signing it and providing any comments
- Following up the review on a regular basis prior to the next performance evaluation

Performance Evaluation Training

A performance evaluation is only as good as those who implement it. Without training, managers and supervisors will be unaware of the problem areas that they should avoid, such as:[3]

1. A tendency toward leniency or harshness that does not produce an accurate measure of the employee's abilities
2. The *halo effect*, the tendency to rate someone highly simply because that particular employee is well-liked or to rate someone poorly because the individual is disliked
3. The *central tendency*, rating all employees as average
4. The *similar to me effect*, evaluating those who are most like the rater highly and those who are not similar to the rater poorly
5. The *most recent error effect*, the tendency to consider not the employee's typical and overall performance but only the employee's most recent performance
6. *Stereotyping*, rating an employee based upon a particular dislike for a particular characteristic of the employee, such as dress style or hair length

Performance Evaluation Uses

Performance evaluations have several uses:[4]

1. Enabling an employee to better understand his or her job and the areas of satisfactory and unsatisfactory performance
2. Providing a supervisor with a formal mechanism by which to review each employee's performance and discuss it with the employee
3. Permitting the supervisor to increase the employee's morale, by complimenting the good aspects of performance,

---

[3] *Id.*

[4] *See* American Hospital Association, The Wrongful Discharge of Employees in the Healthcare Industry 40 (1987).

and to enable the employee to become more efficient, by pointing out weaknesses

4. Minimizing wrongful termination claims over job performance, in that:

   a. A terminated employee who has been counselled and made aware of his or her problems will have a better perception of employer fairness

   b. The employee will know that the employer's case is documented

Performance Evaluation Guidelines
for Supervisors

The following should be reviewed by a supervisor before completing a performance evaluation:

1. Consider the employee's typical performance during the entire period

2. Do not overemphasize recent happenings or isolated incidents that are not typical of the employee's normal performance

3. Use accurate data obtained from records whenever possible, or from careful observation when this is not possible

4. Compare the employee's performance being reviewed with other individuals who have performed the same job

5. Do not let one performance factor influence other factors

6. Each performance factor should be considered independently of the others

7. Do not permit salary or length of service to affect the performance evaluation

8. Consider only the employee's performance in relationship to the specific job requirements

9. Do not rate an employee high because the employee has years of service, but performs at an average rate

10. Do not let personal feelings bias the performance evaluation

11. Do not attribute greater proficiency to personally well-liked employees, or because of sympathy for an employee

12. Do not be wrongly influenced by a prior performance evaluation

PERFORMANCE EVALUATION POLICY

The following policy should be considered as the basis for a performance evaluation system:

PERFORMANCE EVALUATION POLICY[5]

Section 1. Purpose. Frequent communication with employees concerning performance is essential. Ongoing, positive communications can motivate and reinforce outstanding performance, which is the ultimate goal of the Company's performance evaluation system. Also, communications may focus attention on performance which needs improvement. Prompt discussion of a problem situation will help prevent it from becoming a major problem when review time comes several weeks or months later. A good performance evaluation will:

a. Provide the employee with a means of obtaining guidance necessary for maximum growth;

b. Give each supervisor a means of determining the type of management guidance and development the employee needs;

c. Provide direction to assure that the employee's efforts are channeled toward objectives;

d. Give each supervisor the means for analyzing an employee's performance; and

e. Result in more effective work, since people tend to work better if they know what is expected of them and can measure their progress.

Section 2. Requirements. All supervisors are required to conduct performance evaluations and planning sessions as follows:

a. New hires, newly transferred and promoted employees:

  (i)   The first performance evaluation will occur three (3) months after the starting date in the new position.

  (ii) The second performance evaluation will follow three (3) months after the first.

  (iii) The third and subsequent performance reviews should occur on at least an annual basis thereafter.

b. All other employees on annual basis

c. Performance appraisals in addition to these may be initiated by the supervisor where a significant deterioration or improvement in performance warrants deviating from the normal schedule.

Section 3. Procedure. The following procedure will be used for conducting performance evaluations:

a. The Human Resources Department will notify the supervisor approximately one month in advance of the review date, by forwarding a performance evaluation form.

b. The employee's job description is the basic document for the performance evaluation. Before completing the performance evaluation, the supervisor should make sure the job description is current. If necessary, the

---

[5] For an excellent discussion of performance evaluation procedures and policies, *see* Bureau of National Affairs, Inc., Performance Appraisal Programs, PPF Survey No. 135 24–40 (Feb. 1983).

description should be revised to reflect any significant changes in job content.

c. In completing the performance evaluation, the supervisor should review performance of employees against actual accomplishment of duties or accountabilities as set forth in the job position description. Consideration should also be given to employee growth and development and performance improvements that have occurred since the last performance evaluation. This can readily be done by comparing actual results against plans made at the last review.

d. Wherever possible, objective, quantifiable measures should be used to evaluate performance, and specific examples of behavior illustrating performance ratings should be noted on the performance evaluation.

e. Once the performance evaluation is completed, the supervisor must secure the next management level's approval.

f. When the appropriate approvals have been obtained, the original form should be sent to the Human Resources Department to check that the form has been completely and correctly filled out.

g. When the original performance evaluation form is returned from the Human Resources Department, an appointment should be made with the employee to discuss the review. Reasonable advance notice should be given, and the time scheduled should be adequate to allow for a full discussion. The interview itself should be conducted in privacy, without interruptions.

h. During the interview, the supervisor should explain each separate rating individually, using examples to illustrate the performance rating chosen.

i. After completing the review of past performance, the supervisor and the employee should jointly determine development plans and performance goals for the next rating period. *Development plans* identify specific ways in which the employee will try to improve deficient areas or gain additional skills. *Performance goals* are objective, work-oriented targets that both the supervisor and the employee agree are reasonable and realistic given the employee's current performance level, expected improvement, and external factors which may affect accomplishment. The supervisor should guide, rather than dominate, this phase of the review, and should encourage employee participation. Achievement of these plans and goals requires the full acceptance and support of both parties.

j. Once the interview is completed, the supervisor must secure the employee's written acknowledgment of the review and his or her written approval of the development plans and performance goals.

k. The supervisor should then give the employee a photocopy of the development/goals section of the performance evaluation form, and should also keep a photocopy of both for his or her own records. The original performance evaluation, including the development/goals section, should be sent to the Human Resources Department.

Section 4. Definitions. The following definitions should be used when evaluating performance both on an individual accountability and on an overall rating basis:

242

a. *Marginal.* Performance of a fully trained employee does not meet acceptable level; requires improvement. An overall rating of marginal that does not prompt improved performance could result in termination or demotion, and should never result in a salary increase.

b. *Provisional.* Performance does not meet acceptable levels in all areas, but the employee is steadily improving and exhibits the potential to become proficient with continued training. A provisional rating is often given to inexperienced newcomers.

c. *Proficient/Effective.* Performance fully meets standards set for the position on a consistent basis. This should be the expected level of performance in a position. An employee operating at this level of performance is doing a good job.

d. *Superior.* Performance consistently exceeds standards set for the position. Such a performer is normally a seasoned employee.

e. *Outstanding.* Performance so exceeds standards for the position that the excellence of the individual's work is clearly recognized by all. This level of performance is far above the Proficient/Effective level and is normally achieved by only a small percentage of employees.

PERFORMANCE EVALUATION FORM

The following form should be considered in conducting a performance evaluation:[6]

PERFORMANCE EVALUATION

Name

_____

Date

_____

Position Title

_____

Location

_____

Department

_____

PART I—MAJOR POSITION RESPONSIBILITIES

List the significant duties derived from the job description.

_____

_____

_____

_____

_____

_____

PART II—PERFORMANCE OF OBJECTIVES

Summarize below three to five of the most important objectives undertaken since the last performance evaluation, and comment on the results achieved.

Objectives	*Results Achieved*
_____	_____
_____	_____
_____	_____
_____	_____
_____	_____
_____	_____
_____	_____

PERFORMANCE EVALUATION (*Continued*)

PART III—OTHER PERFORMANCE COMMENTS

Difficulties encountered in achieving results, quality and quantity of work produced, and so forth.

_____

_____

_____

_____

_____

_____

_____

_____

_____

PART IV—KNOWLEDGE AND SKILLS

Illustrate and comment on the two or three skill areas in which recent performance indicates high competence or need for improvement.

Demonstrated skills which lead to a high level of performance:

_____

_____

_____

_____

_____

Skills which need improvement (be specific in illustrating how greater skill in these areas could have improved past performance):

_____

_____

_____

_____

PERFORMANCE EVALUATION (*Continued*)

PART V—PERFORMANCE RATING

Considering all aspects of demonstrated job performance, what is the employee's overall rating? (Indicate position in scale.)

Unsatisfactory   _____

Provisional   _____

Acceptable   _____

Fully Satisfactory   _____

Above Expectations   _____

Excellent   _____

PART VI—ACTION PLANS FOR IMPROVING PERFORMANCE IN PRESENT JOB

1. What on-the-job actions will be taken before the next performance evaluation to help the employee improve performance?

Actions to be taken by the employee:

_____

_____

_____

Actions to be taken by the supervisor:

_____

_____

_____

2. Specific training program recommendations:

_____

_____

_____

3. Improvements expected:

_____

_____

_____

PERFORMANCE EVALUATION *(Continued)*

PART VII—OTHER COMMENTS

Record significant points arising from the discussion of the performance evaluation with the employee.

_____

_____

_____

_____

_____

PART VIII

EVALUATION PREPARED BY: _____

SUPERVISOR'S SIGNATURE _____

TITLE _____ DATE _____

CHECK APPROPRIATE LINE:

_____ I have discussed the content of this performance evaluation with my supervisor and I concur with it.

_____ I have reviewed the content of this performance evaluation with my supervisor and I do not concur with it. My comments:

_____ Are attached

_____ Are not attached

_____ Will be submitted later

Employee Signature _____

Date _____

RELIGIOUS ACCOMMODATION

RELIGIOUS ACCOMMODATION PRIVACY PRINCIPLES

Workplace employee privacy interests may arise around religious practices. These result from dress and grooming codes, hours of work requirements, sabbath celebration, union membership, and so forth.

Claims regarding religious accommodation generally involve federal and state FEP statutes. Under the federal Civil Rights Act of 1964 (Title VII), once an employer offers an accommodation to an employee's practice that is reasonable, it has satisfied its duty. It must do so unless accommodation would result in undue hardship to the employer's business.

RELIGIOUS ACCOMMODATION PROCEDURES

The following should be considered in dealing with religious accommodation of employees at the workplace:

1. Where a religious accommodation would affect a collective bargaining agreement's terms, the employer should contact the union.
2. Safety may be evaluated to determine whether the religious accommodation would impose undue employer hardship.
3. Undue hardship may exist where co-workers object to the religious accommodation.
4. Future impact of accommodating an employee's religious belief is insufficient to establish undue hardship.
5. An employee requesting a religious accommodation:
    *   Incurs no liability if he or she refuses to attempt to accommodate or to cooperate.
    *   Must inform the employer that religious beliefs create a problem.
    *   Is not required to suggest possible accommodations.

RELIGIOUS ACCOMMODATION POLICY

The following policy should be considered in dealing with workplace employee religious accommodation:

RELIGIOUS ACCOMMODATION POLICY

The Company or its employees will not discriminate on the basis of an employee's religious belief. Where a workplace religious accommodation is sought, the employee must inform the Company. The Company will use its best efforts to accommodate the employee's religious belief, provided that no undue hardship is created for the Company or its employees and the accommodation does not affect safety or health.

PRIVACY MISCONDUCT

PRIVACY MISCONDUCT PRINCIPLES

Employee privacy interests may be affected by other employees. Other employees may abridge privacy interests present in speech, beliefs, associations, information, and lifestyles. When this occurs, the employer may be obligated to take disciplinary action.

PRIVACY MISCONDUCT PROCEDURES

In developing privacy misconduct procedures, the following should be considered:

1. Employee physical privacy
2. Employee information collection, maintenance, use, and disclosure privacy
3. Applicable federal and state statutes, where employer liability may result from sexual harassment, disclosure of employment records, and so forth

PRIVACY MISCONDUCT POLICY

The following policy should be considered in developing a privacy misconduct policy:

PRIVACY MISCONDUCT POLICY

The Company considers employee privacy to be paramount. The Company along with its employees must ensure this. Physical intrusions of another employee's privacy will not be tolerated. Information will be collected, maintained, used, and disclosed with employee privacy interests protected. Only when a job-related use, a Company business justification, or a governmentally required or court-required disclosure exists, will employee privacy interests be compromised. Failure to follow employee privacy guidelines may result in disciplinary action up to and including termination.

SEXUAL HARASSMENT

SEXUAL HARASSMENT PRIVACY PRINCIPLES

Sexual harassment affects associational and informational interests by creating an offensive workplace environment or by demanding sexual favors in exchange for advantageous workplace treatment. Sexual harassment is generally regulated by federal and state FEP statutes.

To establish sexual harassment, the employee must prove that sexual harassment was based on sex. The employee must have been subject to sexual harassment affecting an employment term, condition, or privilege, and the employer must have known or have been able to know of the harassment and failed to take remedial action.

SEXUAL HARASSMENT PROCEDURES

General Considerations

To respond to and prevent workplace sexual harassment, employers should:

1. Develop a policy that:
    *   Defines sexual harassment
    *   Prohibits sexual harassment
    *   Contains a complaint or grievance procedure where the employee is not required initially to raise the sexual harassment concern with the harasser
    *   Imposes discipline up to and including termination for sexual harassment
2. Discuss sexual harassment concerns at training and supervisor meetings
3. Investigate all sexual harassment complaints

Sexual Harassment Investigation

The following procedure should be considered for use in employee sexual harassment claim investigations:

1. Upon receiving a sexual harassment complaint, the human resources staff should:

- Discuss it with the employee
- Advise the employee that, because of sexual harassment's sensitive nature, the complaint should not be discussed with co-workers or others
- Interview the alleged harasser
- Maintain confidentiality
- Interview other persons with pertinent information; that is, witnesses or persons who also have had problems with the alleged harasser
- Inform or reiterate to the alleged harasser the sexual harassment policy
- Advise a supervisor, where he or she should be advised, that retaliation against the complaining employee is prohibited
- Hold a group meeting to discuss the problem, when an unknown person is causing the harassment

2. Should it be determined that sexual harassment occurred, appropriate discipline up to and including termination should be imposed
3. Upon concluding the human resources staff's investigation, the complainant should be contacted to:
   - Explain what action has been taken
   - Request the complainant to report other sexual harassment occurrences
   - Reiterate that the employer forbids sexual harassment
   - Reinforce the policy that employees with sexual harassment complaints are to inform management of these instances immediately

SEXUAL HARASSMENT POLICY

The following policy should be considered concerning sexual harassment:[7]

---

[7] For an excellent discussion of sexual harassment procedures and policies, *see* Bureau of National Affairs, Inc., Sexual Harassment: Employer Policies and Problems, PPF Survey No. 144 (June 1987).

SEXUAL HARASSMENT POLICY

Section 1. Purpose. To provide a work environment free from all forms of sexual harassment or intimidation.

Section 2. Policy. It is the Company's policy to regard sexual harassment as a very serious matter and to prohibit it in the workplace by any person and in any form.

Section 3. Procedure.

a. Each supervisor has an affirmative duty to maintain his or her workplace free from sexual harassment.

b. Each supervisor shall discuss this policy with all employees and assure them that they are not required to endure insulting, degrading, or exploitative sexual harassment.

c. No supervisor shall threaten or insinuate, either explicitly or implicitly, that an employee's refusal to submit to sexual advances will adversely affect the employee's employment, evaluation, wages, advancement, assigned duties, shifts, other conditions of employment, career development, and so forth.

d. Other sexually harassing conduct in the workplace, whether committed by supervisors or nonsupervisory personnel, is also prohibited, including:

   (i)   Unwelcome sexual flirtations, advances, or propositions;
   (ii)   Verbal or written abuse of a sexual nature;
   (iii) Graphic verbal comments about an individual's body;
   (iv)   Sexually degrading words used to describe an individual; and
   (v)   The display in the workplace of sexually suggestive objects or pictures.

e. Any employee who believes he or she has been sexually harassed should report the alleged act immediately to the Human Resources Department. If the complaint involves someone in the employee's direct line of supervision, then the employee should inform another supervisor of the complaint. The complaint will be investigated by the Human Resources Department and the employee will be advised of the findings and conclusion.

f. There will be no discrimination or retaliation against any employee for making a sexual harassment complaint.

g. All actions taken to resolve sexual harassment complaints through internal investigations shall be conducted confidentially.

h. Any supervisor, agent, or other employee who is found, after appropriate investigation, to have engaged in sexual harassment will be subject to appropriate disciplinary action up to and including termination.

SEXUAL HARASSMENT: CONFIDENTIALITY

The following should be considered in stressing that confidentiality will be preserved for sexual harassment complaints:

SEXUAL HARASSMENT: CONFIDENTIALITY

Section 1. Complaints. All employees are responsible for assuring that the workplace is free from sexual harassment. Any employee who has a workplace sexual harassment complaint, including supervisors, co-workers, or visitors, must bring the problem to the Company's attention. IF THE COMPLAINT INVOLVES SOMEONE IN THE EMPLOYEE'S DIRECT LINE OF SUPERVISION, THEN THE EMPLOYEE SHOULD INFORM ANOTHER SUPERVISOR OF THE COMPLAINT.

Section 2. Complaint Confidentiality. All complaints will be promptly handled and special privacy safeguards will be applied in handling sexual harassment complaints. All employees should be aware that the identities of the complaining party and the person accused of sexual harassment will be kept confidential. The Company will retain confidential documentation of all allegations and investigations and will take appropriate corrective action, including discipline up to and including termination.

SEXUAL HARASSMENT COMPLAINT FORM

The following form should be considered in reporting sexual harassment incidents:[8]

---

[8] For more specifics regarding reporting sexual harassment, *see* Bureau of National Affairs, Inc., Sexual Harassment: Employer Policies and Problems, PPF survey No. 144, at 46–47 (June 1987).

SEXUAL HARASSMENT COMPLAINT FORM

Name: _____

Position: _____

Department: _____

Shift: _____

Immediate Supervisor: _____

1. Describe the sexual harassment incident.

_____

_____

_____

_____

_____

_____

2. Who was responsible for the sexual harassment?

_____

_____

_____

_____

_____

_____

_____

3. List any witnesses to the sexual harassment incident.

_____

_____

_____

_____

_____

_____

_____

SEXUAL HARASSMENT COMPLAINT FORM *(Continued)*

4. Where did the sexual harassment take place?

_____

_____

_____

_____

_____

_____

5. Identify the date(s) and time(s) that the sexual harassment occurred.

_____

_____

_____

_____

_____

_____

_____

_____

_____   _____

       Employee   Date

RESTRICTIVE COVENANTS

RESTRICTIVE COVENANT PRIVACY PRINCIPLES

Restrictive covenants generally involve employee responsibilities toward the employer during and after employment termination. These responsibilities usually involve covenants not to compete, customer lists, and trade secrets. They are often found in written employment contracts.

These covenants impact employee privacy by limiting employee opportunities and curtailing use of inventions, products, information, and knowledge developed, learned, or obtained by the employee at the workplace. They restrict the geographical area where similar employment may be located. Time limitations are also included to restrict the employee's ability to engage, use, or exercise these opportunities.

When supported by consideration ancillary to a lawful contract, along with being reasonable and consistent with the public interest, these covenants are enforceable. Subject matter covered by these covenants includes the employee's commitment not to compete with the former employer for a specified time period within a certain geographical territory; disclosure of customer lists, information and data; disclosure of trade secrets learned during the course of employment; and granting the employer sole rights to inventions, products, and information developed during employment.

To be enforceable, a postemployment restraint must reasonably:

1. Protect a legitimate employer interest
2. Be limited in duration and area
3. Be reasonable in terms of the activities prohibited.

Reasonableness of the covenant is determined by reviewing the employer interest sought to be protected. Generally, the employer's need for protection is balanced against the hardship imposed on the employee. The subject matter of restrictive covenants may be implemented by the employer as part of a written employment contract or an employment policy.

RESTRICTIVE COVENANT PROCEDURES

Restrictive covenants are so varied and complex that no set of procedures can completely protect the employer. However, the following should be considered in minimizing unfair competition by present and former employees:[9]

1. When reviewing the advisability of requiring employees to sign a restrictive covenant:
    - Avoid imposing an overbroad covenant on all employees without distinction
    - Remember that restrictive covenants are not appropriate for every employee, and extremely broad covenants may be held unenforceable as an improper trade restraint
    - Consider that a narrow covenant tailored to key employees may deter the threat of trade secret misappropriation
2. Promulgate a written policy on confidentiality that:
    - Includes a statement on the confidential nature of certain business information
    - Avoids broad statements that all business information is confidential
    - Tailors the policy to meet the needs of the business
3. Preserve the confidentiality of critical business information by:
    - Stamping confidential documents "confidential" and keeping them in a secure place
    - Restricting the circulation of confidential information on a need-to-know basis
    - Not giving suppliers or customers unlimited access to trade secrets
    - Considering written agreements protecting the business from unauthorized disclosure where access is unavoidable
    - Restricting access to parts of the facility where trade secret information is kept
    - Using sign-in and sign-out logs, badges, and so forth
4. Whether information can be protected depends upon:
    - Information knowledge outside the employer's business
    - Information knowledge among employees
    - Employer measures to protect information secrecy

[9] See Murphy, *Investigating, Handling, and Protecting Against Employee Theft and Dishonesty*, in Employment Problems in the Workplace 13, 35-38 (J. Kauff ed. 1986).

- Information value to the employer and competitors
- Effort and money expended by the employer in developing information
- Difficulty for others to acquire or duplicate the information

5. Examples of protectible information:
   - Customer lists
   - Formulas, processes, techniques

6. One step to protect trade secrets and confidential information includes considering a formal employment contract:
   - The employment contract usually is not necessary where an employer wants only to ensure that an employee respects proprietary information confidentiality, or to ensure that the employer will receive the benefit of any inventions the employee creates on employer time
   - If the objective is to keep the employee from competing with the employer or working for a competitor, then an employment contract is probably necessary
   - Noncompetition provisions are more likely to be enforceable when coupled with an agreement for continued employment than when they stand alone and restrict the employee without giving the employee assurance of continued employment or pay

RESTRICTIVE COVENANT POLICIES[10]

The following policies are not intended to constitute separate or independent employment contracts. Before using these policies for this purpose, there are contract and employment matters that must be evaluated. For example, it may be necessary to provide additional consideration if current employees are requested to enter into agreements containing restrictive covenants.

[10] For additional information regarding restrictive covenants and their application, *see* Littler, Mendelson, Fastiff & Tichy, *Preventing Unfair Competition: Protecting Trade Secrets, and Enforcing Covenants Not to Compete,* in the 1987 Employer I (1987). Littler, Mendelson, Fastiff, Tichy prepare this publication on an annual basis for Business Laws, Inc. of 8288 Mayfield Road in Chesterland, Ohio 44026; telephone (216) 729-7996. As an annual update of employment laws, this is an excellent reference source for human resource professionals and attorneys.

Confidential Information Policy

The following policy should be considered regarding maintaining confidential information:

CONFIDENTIAL INFORMATION POLICY

From time to time an employee may have access to confidential information involving Company affairs, customers' advertising, news stories prior to their release dates, and so forth. Unauthorized disclosure of this information is detrimental to the Company. At no time should an employee knowingly discuss the contents of or remove from the Company's premises this information. Confidential information must be kept confidential. Failure to maintain confidential information may result in an employee's discipline up to and including termination.

Policy Not to Disclose or Use Trade Secrets

The following policy should be considered regarding employee trade secret disclosure:[11]

---

[11] *See id.* at I-14.

POLICY NOT TO DISCLOSE OR USE
TRADE SECRETS

While employed with the Company, employees will have access to and become acquainted with information of a confidential, proprietary, or secret nature. This information is or may be applicable to or related to the Company's present or future business, research, development, investigation, or the business of any Company customer. Trade secret information includes, but is not limited to devices, secret inventions, processes, compilations of information, records, specifications, and information concerning customers or vendors. Employees shall not disclose any Company trade secrets directly or indirectly, use them in any way, either during the term of their employment or at any time thereafter, except as required in the course of Company employment.

No Solicitation of Customers Policy

> The following policy should be considered regarding deterring the solicitation of customers by employees:[12]

NO SOLICITATION OF CUSTOMERS POLICY

As an employment condition, all Company customers that employees now or hereafter service during their employment, and all prospective customers from whom employees have solicited business while in the Company's employ, shall be solely the Company's customers. For a period of one year immediately following employment termination, employees shall not, either directly or indirectly, solicit business regarding products or services competitive with those of the Company from any of the Company's customers with whom employees had contact within one year prior to the employees' termination within the following geographical area. (Describe area in specifics.)

[12] *See id.* at I-15 to I-16.

No Solicitation of Employee Policy

> The following policy should be considered regarding deterring employees from soliciting fellow employees for other employment:[13]

NO SOLICITATION OF EMPLOYEES' POLICY

As an employment condition, employees agree that the Company has invested substantial time and effort in assembling its present workforce. For a period of one year after employment termination, employees will not, directly or indirectly, induce or solicit any of the Company's employees to leave their employment.

Disclosure and Assignment of Invention Policy

> The following policy should be considered regarding disclosure and assignment of invention:[14]

DISCLOSURE AND ASSIGNMENT OF INVENTION POLICY

As an employment condition, employees agree to disclose to the Company any and all inventions, discoveries, improvements, trade secrets, formulas, techniques, processes, know-how, and so forth, whether or not patentable and whether or not made or conceived by them, either solely or in conjunction with others, during their employment, which relate to or result from the actual or anticipated business, work, or research in development of the Company, and which result, to any extent, from use of the Company's premises or property, or are suggested by any task assigned to them or any work performed by them for or on the Company's behalf. Employees acknowledge and agree that all of these inventions shall be the Company's sole property and employees hereby assign to the Company their entire rights and interests in any inventions.

[13] *See id.* at I-16.
[14] *See id.* at I-16 to I-17.

8

PRIVACY OUTSIDE THE WORKPLACE

Even though workplace commitments are completed, the employee may be subject to privacy intrusions outside the workplace. Depending upon the employer's business and the employee's position, an employer may attempt to hold the employee accountable for or restrict the employee's activities outside the workplace.

Employee associations, financial arrangements, other employment opportunities, living arrangements, romantic involvements, and so forth may be affected by employer-imposed limitations. Privacy concerns arise over whether activities outside the workplace are strictly a personal employee matter, subject only to violation of a law that should be dealt with by the courts, or involve legitimate employer interests.

It is not always clear when an employer may regulate or be concerned with employee activities outside the workplace. Generally, the employer can hold an employee accountable for and limit outside pursuits that are directly related to employment. This chapter reviews policies and procedures relating to outside employment, loyalty, conflicts of interest, noncriminal misconduct, criminal misconduct, and residency requirements.

OUTSIDE EMPLOYMENT

OUTSIDE EMPLOYMENT PRIVACY PRINCIPLES

Employees who hold other jobs, in addition to their primary positions, are becoming increasingly common at virtually all workforce levels. Holding another job while working for an employer, or *moonlighting,* is not by itself subject to employer regulation. Only when the other job interferes with performance, work attendance, or affects the employer economically may it be legitimately regulated.

The primary employer's concern is whether employees are devoting appropriate efforts to their work and whether the secondary job presents a breach of loyalty, a conflict of interest, or threat to the primary employer's business interest, in order to justify a prohibition against other employment. Each instance must be decided on its own facts.

OUTSIDE EMPLOYMENT PROCEDURES

Employees are expected to devote their primary work efforts to the primary employer's business. For employers to restrict or limit outside employment, the following should be considered:

1. Depriving the employer of legitimate business opportunities
2. Derogatory effect on the employer
3. Inconsistency with the employer's interests
4. Devoting time and effort to the additional job such that performance on the primary job is adversely affected

OUTSIDE EMPLOYMENT POLICIES

Outside Employment Prohibited Policy

The following policy should be adopted where it is determined that all outside employment should be prohibited for legitimate job-related business interests:

OUTSIDE EMPLOYMENT PROHIBITED POLICY

The Company will not knowingly hire or retain any person who is otherwise employed. While employed with the Company no employee will be permitted to hold outside employment.

Outside Employment Discouraged Policy

The following policy should be adopted where it has been determined that not all outside employment should be prohibited, but that certain outside employment should be discouraged to protect legitimate job-related business interests:

OUTSIDE EMPLOYMENT DISCOURAGED POLICY

The Company does not encourage employment in other part-time or full-time employment or owning and conducting another business. Outside employment is considered to be undesirable because it may adversely affect an employee's job performance with the Company.

Outside Employment Conflict of Interest Policy

The following policy should be adopted where it has been determined that outside employment is permitted unless it is a conflict of interest or interferes with the primary employment:

OUTSIDE EMPLOYMENT CONFLICT OF INTEREST POLICY

Employees may engage in outside employment provided it does not interfere with their job performance and that it is not with another employer who competes with the Company. No employee shall use his or her position with the Company to exploit outside employment interests. Employees engaged in outside employment must immediately inform their supervisors.

Outside Employment Interfering with Performance Policy

The following policy should be adopted where it has been determined that outside employment is permitted unless it interferes with employee job performance:

OUTSIDE EMPLOYMENT INTERFERING WITH PERFORMANCE POLICY

Company employment shall be considered the employee's primary employment. Compensated outside employment shall be limited so as not to impair employee job performance. Should there be a conflict in employment, the supervisor, along with the Human Resources Department, shall review the problem. If the dispute cannot be resolved, the employee may be required to discontinue outside employment or be subject to employment separation.

Outside Employment Disclosure Policy

The following policy should be adopted where outside employment is permitted provided that it is disclosed and does not interfere with legitimate job-related business interests:

OUTSIDE EMPLOYMENT DISCLOSURE POLICY

Employees may engage in outside employment as long as this is disclosed and is determined by the Company not to interfere with the employee's full-time job performance. Each employee must disclose in writing all outside employment. Failure to disclose outside employment or a misrepresentation of outside employment may result in disciplinary action up to and including termination.

Outside Employment Approval Policy

The following policy should be adopted where outside employment is permitted with the employer's approval.

OUTSIDE EMPLOYMENT APPROVAL POLICY

Employees desiring to engage in or who are engaged in outside employment must advise the Company of this in writing. Outside employment may not be entered into or continued unless authorized by the Company in writing.

LOYALTY

LOYALTY PRIVACY PRINCIPLES

As a privacy interest, every employee impliedly promises to serve the employer faithfully and honestly. A significant privacy concern arises over the employer's right to demand loyalty outside the workplace, in that this affects the employee's furtherance of association and economic opportunities.

Loyalty is owed by employees to their employers even though they may not be officers or directors. The employment relationship may be terminated if the employee fails to serve the employer loyally. Termination normally occurs when an employee engages in outside business activities resulting in less work for the employer, or attempts to interfere with the employer's business or customers. Loyalty problems may arise out of embezzling employer funds, appropriating the employer's business opportunities, encouraging other employees to terminate employment, planning to begin another business while an employee, or carrying out other employment preparations on the current employer's working time.

LOYALTY PROCEDURES

The following effects of outside or secondary employment would be problematic:

1. Depriving the employer of legitimate business opportunities
2. Derogatory effect on the employer
3. Inconsistency with the employer's interests
4. Devoting time and effort to the additional job such that performance on the primary job is adversely affected

LOYALTY POLICY

The following policy should be adopted in notifying employees of their primary interest in loyally furthering the employer's legitimate job-related business interests:

LOYALTY POLICY

Employees shall not engage directly or indirectly in any outside relationship or activity that defers or would adversely affect their primary responsibility, interest, duty, or loyalty in actively furthering the Company's business.

CONFLICTS OF INTEREST

CONFLICT OF INTEREST PRIVACY PRINCIPLES

The previous discussion involved the employee's duty to avoid or disclose any actual or possible conflict of interest affecting their employer. Often it is not the conflict itself that results in problems but the failure to disclose or to divest the conflict when warned. Termination may be proper where an employee fails to disclose the conflict.

CONFLICT OF INTEREST PROCEDURES

The following should be considered regarding whether outside employment constitutes a conflict of interest:

1. Depriving the employer of legitimate business opportunities
2. Inconsistency with the employer's interests
3. Derogatory effect on the employer
4. Devoting time and effort to the additional job such that performance on the primary job is adversely affected

CONFLICT OF INTEREST POLICIES

Conflict of Interest: Private Employer

The following should be considered by a private employer in developing a conflict of interest policy:

CONFLICT OF INTEREST POLICY

Section 1. **Adverse Pecuniary Interest.** No employee shall:

a. Engage directly or indirectly in any business transactions or private arrangement for profit that accrues from or is based upon his or her position or authority with the Company; or
b. Participate in the negotiation of or decision to award contracts, the settlement of any claims or charges in any contracts, the making of loans, rate fixing, guarantees, or other things of value with or for any entity in which he or she has a financial or personal interest.

Section 2. **Misuse of Information.** No employee may for his or her own personal gain or for the gain of others, use any information obtained as a result of employment and not generally available to the public, or may disclose this information.

Section 3. **Misuse of Company Facilities and Equipment.** No employee shall use any Company equipment, supplies, or properties for his or her own private gain for other than Company-designated and authorized purposes.

Section 4. **Outside Employment.** No employee shall engage in or accept outside employment or render services for another unless this outside employment or service is approved in advance and in writing by the Company.

Section 5. **Violation.** Employees who refuse or fail to comply with the policies set forth herein may be subject to disciplinary action including, but not limited to, reprimands, suspensions, and termination.

NONCRIMINAL MISCONDUCT

NONCRIMINAL MISCONDUCT PRIVACY PRINCIPLES

Employee misconduct outside the workplace may affect the employment relationship. Where the misconduct directly relates to the employment relationship and affects it, the employer's concern may be legitimate.

Certain instances arise where the employer may properly demonstrate concern for employee misconduct outside the workplace, and may impose discipline up to and including termination. Fights outside the workplace over personal matters would not normally be subject to employer regulation. Where the fight relates to the employment relationship and affects the work environment, the employer's concern may be legitimate.

The difficulty arises in determining when an employee's privacy interests must yield to the employer's legitimate business interests. Employers generally must maintain that the employee's misconduct outside the workplace caused an actual business loss or injured the employer's reputation.

A bus operator was properly terminated when he was publicly identified as the acting grand dragon of the Ku Klux Klan. A danger of physical violence existed, along with a threatened employee wildcat strike and an economic boycott. The employee's activities, not beliefs, were at issue.

NONCRIMINAL MISCONDUCT PROCEDURES

The following should be considered regarding noncriminal misconduct that occurs outside the workplace:

1. Injurious effect upon the employer's reputation
2. The source and degree of adverse publicity
3. The type of misconduct
4. The employee's position

OFF-DUTY NONCRIMINAL MISCONDUCT POLICY

The following policy should be considered by employers in dealing with noncriminal misconduct arising outside the workplace:

OFF-DUTY NONCRIMINAL MISCONDUCT POLICY

Section 1.   Off-Duty Noncriminal Misconduct.   Noncriminal employee misconduct arising outside the workplace may result in disciplinary action up to and including termination depending upon the nature of the conduct and its adverse impact upon the Company's business.

Section 2.   Determination.   Among other factors, the following should be considered in making any disciplinary determination for incidents involving off-duty noncriminal misconduct:

a.   The nature of the off-duty noncriminal misconduct;

b.   The employee's explanation, if available;

c.   The extent to which allowing the employee to continue in his or her position would be detrimental to the physical well-being of the employee, his or her fellow employees, or other persons;

d.   The nature of the employee's job duties, including responsibility and the discretion that must be exercised as part of those duties;

e.   The extent to which the employee must deal directly with the public; and

f.   Any undue hardship to the employee which would result from his or her temporary reassignment.

CRIMINAL MISCONDUCT

Off-duty misconduct involving an arrest or conviction can result in disciplinary action by an employer. When an arrest or conviction has an adverse impact on the employer's business, disciplinary action is generally considered appropriate. The effect and likelihood of negative publicity, along with the sensitive nature of certain positions, makes it likely that criminal activities outside the workplace of employees will have an indirect but damaging impact on the employer's business.

Arrest, indictment, or conviction for employee activity outside the workplace that adversely affects an employee's own or fellow employees' job performance, or is directly or indirectly detrimental to the employer's business, may sustain disciplinary action. This occurred, for example, where a dairy driver-salesman was one of ten people arrested in a raid on a night club and charged with Sunday liquor sale, prostitution, pandering, and conducting obscene exhibitions involving men and women. The employee's suspension was sustained, pending the trial's outcome, because of possible damage to the employer's image and good will. The driver-salesman's duties necessitated a close personal relationship with customers and the charges' seriousness increased the employer's potential harm.

CRIMINAL MISCONDUCT PROCEDURES

The following should be considered regarding criminal misconduct outside the workplace:

1. Negative oral or written publicity
2. Nature of the employee's misconduct
3. Nature of the criminal misconduct; such as arrest, indictment, or conviction
4. Effect on the employee's or fellow employee's job performance
5. Detriment to the employer's business
6. The employee's explanation, if any

CRIMINAL MISCONDUCT POLICY

The following policy should be considered by private employers in dealing with criminal misconduct arising outside the workplace:

CRIMINAL MISCONDUCT POLICY

Section 1. Criminal Conduct Constituting a Felony or Related to Employment. As soon as practicable after an employee has been formally charged with criminal conduct related to his or her employment, or which constitutes a felony, the employee shall be suspended without pay. If the charge results in a conviction in a court of law, the employee shall be terminated.

Section 2. Criminal Conduct Other than a Felony or Not Related to Employment. As soon as practicable after an employee is formally charged with criminal conduct other than a felony, and not related to his or her employment, the Human Resources Department shall conduct an inquiry and make a preliminary determination regarding whether or not the employee should continue to perform his or her duties pending the investigation's outcome and final determination under Section 3 (Investigation) and Section 4 (Final Determination) as follows:

a. *Purpose.* The purpose of the preliminary determination is to minimize the effect which the accusation of a crime by an employee may have upon the Company's ability to function, pending an investigation and final determination regarding the existence of sufficient reason for employee disciplinary action.

b. *Making the Preliminary Determination.* In making a preliminary determination, the Human Resources Department shall select one of the following alternatives and implement it:

   (i)   Allow the employee to continue to perform duties pending the investigation's outcome and final determination;
   (ii) Reassign the employee to less sensitive duties within the Company pending the investigation's outcome and final determination; or
   (iii) Suspend the employee without pay pending the investigation's outcome and final determination.

c. *Factors to Be Considered in Making the Preliminary Determination.* In making the preliminary determination, the Human Resources Department shall consider, among other factors, the following:

   (i)   The employee's explanation, if available;
   (ii)   The extent to which allowing the employee to continue in his or her position would be detrimental to the employee's physical well-being, his or her fellow workers, or other persons;
   (iii) The nature of the employee's duties, including the discretion exercised as part of those duties;
   (iv)   The nature, weight, basis, and source of the accusations against the employee;
   (v)   The accusations' relationship to the employee's duties;
   (vi)   The extent to which the employee must deal directly with the public; and
   (vii) Any undue hardship to the employee that would result from a temporary reassignment.

d. *Contact with Law Enforcement Agency.* In considering the nature, weight, and source of the accusations against an employee, the Company shall contact the law enforcement agency involved in the accusations against the employee to verify the charge and to obtain all available information.

e. *Employee Status.* After the preliminary determination is made, the employee shall remain in the status selected pending the investigation's outcome and final determination under Sections 3 (Investigation) and 4 (Final Determination). This status shall be temporary pending the outcome of the investigation by the Human Resources Department, and shall not bear upon the final determination.

Section 3. Investigation. Any employee formally charged with criminal conduct shall be subject to an immediate investigation conducted by the Human Resources Department:

a. *Purpose.* The investigation's purpose shall be to determine whether sufficient reason exists for disciplinary action including, but not limited to, suspension, demotion, or termination.

b. *Conduct of Investigation.* In the investigation, all the relevant facts shall be promptly gathered and considered. The investigation shall be completed within 12 working days. The following may be considered:

  (i) *Law Enforcement Agencies.* The Human Resources Department may request the assistance of any law enforcement agency involved in the matter; however, this shall not relieve the Human Resources Department of the responsibility to make an independent evaluation.

  (ii) *Employee Contact.* The Human Resources Department shall afford the employee an opportunity to explain the accusations and the opportunity to have representation during meetings relating to the investigation, if representation is requested, and the opportunity to submit additional information.

Section 4. Final Determination. After completion of the investigation, the Human Resources Department shall have five working days to make a final determination as to whether the investigation's results establish sufficient reason for disciplinary action and, if established, what disciplinary action should be taken. The Company's President shall review this decision and ratify the Human Resources Department's decision, absent an abuse of discretion. In determining whether sufficient reason for disciplinary action exists, the Human Resources Department shall consider, among other factors:

a. The employee's explanation, if available;

b. The extent to which allowing the employee to continue in his or her position would be detrimental to the employee's physical well-being, his or her fellow workers, or other persons;

c. The nature of the employee's duties, including the amount of discretion exercised as part of those duties;

d. The nature, weight, and source of the accusations against the employee;

e.   The accusations' relationship to the employee's duties; and

f.   The extent to which the employee must deal with the public.

Where sufficient reason for disciplinary action exists, the Human Resources Department shall immediately take appropriate disciplinary action including, but not limited to, suspension, demotion, or termination, which action shall be reviewed by the Company's President and ratified by him or her absent an abuse of discretion. If, based on information available at that time, a finding of sufficient reason is not made, the employee shall be notified of the disposition and shall retain or be retroactively reinstated to his or her previous position.

RESIDENCY REQUIREMENTS

RESIDENCY PRIVACY PRINCIPLES

Employer residency regulation affects associational privacy interests. At issue in residency requirements are employee privacy interests in choosing where to live, a right to travel, and geographical limits curtailing access to employment opportunities.

Residency requirements necessary to serve legitimate employer interests are valid. Generally, a person's *residence* is where he or she lives and where he or she intends to stay, that is, the domicile or abode. Physical presence for a long time period is not dispositive of residence. Other factors include:

1. Voting place
2. Mailing address
3. Driver's license address
4. Where one keeps clothing
5. Location of property owned
6. Rental payment

Public employment positions involving teachers, police, and firefighters are frequently the subject of residency requirements. However, in one case in which a collective bargaining agreement recognized the employer's right to establish reasonable rules and regulations for the safe and efficient conduct of the city's business, a residency requirement was held to be unreasonable because a three-mile restriction could not be justified.

RESIDENCY PROCEDURES

Residency procedures should:

1. Have a practical justification where they require employees to live within a convenient distance from their work to facilitate emergency callbacks
2. Be based upon a legitimate job-related desire to have the employee involved in the community's affairs
3. Require the employee to meet the residency requirement within a certain time limit

RESIDENCY POLICY

The following policy should be considered where a residency requirement is desired:

RESIDENCY POLICY

Section 1. Residence. Residence is the place or locality where an employee lives and has manifested an intent to continue to live. Factors providing evidence of intent to maintain residency include the following:

a. Rent, lease, or purchase of a property that the employee has made his or her home;
b. Payment of State and local taxes;
c. Registration of personal property including bank accounts, stocks, bonds, and automobiles within ___(State's name)__;
d. Possession of a current ___(State's name)___ motor vehicle operator's license; or
e. Current registration to vote in ___(State's name)__.

Section 2. Application. Residency requirements shall be as follows:

a. Persons hired shall be legal residents of this State, unless residence has been waived, and shall reside within ___(Describe area)__.
b. The Director of Personnel, upon submission of satisfactory justification, may limit hiring to those who are residents of this State who must reside within ___(Describe area)__.

Section 3. Waiver. When it appears that there is an inadequate supply of well-qualified residents within the ___(Describe area)___ available for a particular position, the Director of Personnel may waive the residency requirement.

INDEX